Ultimate Success

Success

Laying Up Your Treasures in Heaven

Ultimate
Success

*Laying Up Your Treasures
in Heaven*

David Shibley

New Leaf Press

CONTENTS

To my parents

Lillian Shibley
living with us in Texas
and
Warren Shibley
living with Jesus in heaven.

They taught me
to seek another world.

Foreword

However this book happened into your hands, I can assure you that you're about to encounter a life-enriching experience.

If you happened to purchase it, you'll soon consider your purchase one of the best investments you've ever made. If it was given to you as a gift, I'm sure you will forever thank the giver.

Indeed, *Ultimate Success* is the kind of book one needs to read at least once a year just to keep in focus the real issues of life — eternal life, that is.

I had read only a few pages of David Shibley's timely challenge when the thought flashed through my mind: *This is must reading for my daughters.* I honestly could not remember reading, in years, a devotional book about which I felt this more strongly. And the more I read, the more I realized how truly essential this message is.

This book is, in my opinion, must reading for every believer who wonders what God is trying to say to a troubled Church in an age of misguided priorities.

For me, *Ultimate Success* has brought back into focus what really matters in life — living for Jesus with an eye on eternity. It has filled my heart with a renewed anticipation of the joys of heaven and the hope of eternity that awaits every follower of Jesus Christ.

Beloved reader, I pray as I write these words that the

life-changing insights you're about to uncover will challenge your heart as powerfully as they have mine.

Together let us face each tomorrow with the hope of a heaven that is infinitely real and eternally ours. Because best of all, Jesus is already there!

Dick Eastman
President
Every Home for Christ
Colorado Springs, Colorado

Introduction

We are entering a time when many in our nation are recognizing the shallowness of a protectionist mentality. There is an inner longing for something deeper. The pensive Christian dares to believe this is an innate desire to please God.

For too long we have preached and lived a pseudo-gospel that suggested every person could do what seemed right in his own eyes. Now, amid the agony of our self-inflicted wounds, God is lovingly wooing us back to accountability — to Him and to each other.

For such healthy readjustment to occur, we must first have a new perception of things. Much of the Church has both swallowed and been swallowed by forms of existentialism. Now the pendulum needs to swing back to an eternity-oriented message. And such a message demands some fresh definitions, particularly when it comes to success. Dietrich Bonhoeffer, who died in a Nazi prison camp, said, "The figure of the Crucified invalidates all thought that takes success for its standard." Prayerfully, we are entering an era when the standard is not success but obedience. This book is a call to that kind of mental and spiritual realignment. Pleasing Jesus brings ultimate success and fulfillment.

New goals, then, are in order. Our hearts' desires must come into line with His. Living in the light of our sure appointment with Him brings a new set of drives; the only "well done" that really matters is His. This releases the heavenly minded Christian to incredible freedom now, in this life.

The thrust of this book is to pull us back to the historic emphasis the Christian faith has always given to heaven and its rewards. Because of our colossal neglect of this area in recent years, a Scripture guide and bibliography have been provided for further study. It's high time we understand what it means to live in the light of eternity.

I could never properly acknowledge all the friends, teachers, and co-workers in ministry who have helped me have a heart turned toward eternity. But I do express my indebtedness to each one. I'm especially grateful for the support of my family. Naomi, Jonathan, and Joel have helped pray this book into reality.

One hundred years ago Henry Ward Beecher expressed a yearning for the afterlife. "I have drunk at many a fountain, but thirst came again. I have fed at many a bounteous table, but hunger returned. I have seen many bright and lovely things, but, while I gazed, their luster faded. There is nothing here that can give me rest; but when I behold Thee, O God, I shall be satisfied!" The heart's eternal longings can be assuaged only by that which is eternal.

Soon we will stand before Christ to give an account for our stewardship and to receive any rewards we may have won. May Jude's benediction to his readers grace your heart as you read these pages and prepare for that day: "Now to Him who is able to keep you from stumbling, and to present you faultless before the presence of His glory with exceeding joy, to God our Savior, who alone is wise, be glory and majesty, dominion and power, both now and forever. Amen" (Jude 24).

— David Shibley

Ten thousand times ten thousand
In sparkling raiment bright,
The armies of the ransomed saints
Throng up the steeps of light:
'Tis finished, all is finished,
Their fight with death and sin:
Fling open wide the golden gates,
And let the victors in.

— Henry Alford, 1867

1

A Call to Ultimate Success

He has also set eternity in the hearts of men
. . . (Eccles. 3:11;NIV).

For most Americans, October 23, 1983, is a day that will live in infamy. On that ghastly afternoon a group of terrorists loaded their car with explosives and sped through the barricades of the U.S. Marine compound in Beirut. Seconds later 241 American soldiers died with them beneath a horrific tomb of twisted steel and cement.

How could these fanatics have committed such an act of barbarism? Why did they do it? What would possess them to execute this 1980s version of a kamikaze raid?

The answer, if there is one, is complex. One thing, however, should be understood. Their motive was not merely political: it was theological. Their misguided beliefs assured them that they, in fact, were rendering a service for God by helping to destroy "the great Satan," the United States. For sacrificing their lives in the act of "bravery" they would be richly rewarded. You see, these men who much of the world perceives as lunatics were acting on a belief that was fully logical to them. They were convinced that upon death, they would be immediately ushered into an eternal harem with an endless supply of food and sensual pleasures. Not such a bad deal for someone who is hungry and rejected.

It is not surprising that many American diplomats throw up their hands in despair when attempting to negotiate with leaders from the Middle East. Yet there is really no mystery here. The problem is not so much a failure to perceive motives. The Westerner, more often than not, views life with a secular mindset. He lives for the present and see his rewards as temporal things like accolades from important people and better work compensations. The Middle Easterner, on the other hand, nurtures a theological frame of mind. He lives for the hereafter. He is far more concerned with approval from God than from people. His idea of true upward mobility is his hope for an eternal paradise that, for him, is as real as current hostilities.

Most Americans reject acts of terrorism done in the name of God as unspeakably perverse. Christians in particular find it foreign to all that the Bible stands for. They realize that, if God needs any avenging, He is surely capable of undertaking it himself. "Vengeance is mine, I will repay, says the Lord" (Rom. 12:19). To perpetrate death and destruction in God's name is not an expression of His will; rather it is an insult to His very nature.

Yet we dare not miss the deeper point in all of this. People throughout the world are willing to die — not only for beliefs they hold dear, but for the prospect of lavish compensation in the afterlife. And this concept is *not* foreign to Christianity.

The Missing Factor

To those familiar with scriptural incentives, the prospect of spending eternity with the Lord and being rewarded by Him is one of life's highest motivations. That is, it should be. In actual practice, however, we are not being taught about eternity. Nor are we exhorted to godly living in light of our accountability when we stand before Jesus Christ.

Think about it. When was the last time you heard a minister speak of a home in heaven and rescue from perdition as being as vital as freedom from guilt or a new start in life?

Judson Cornwall said, "It has been many years since I have heard a Christian testify to homesickness for heaven, and even longer since I have heard a sermon extolling the joys of heaven. Perhaps it is because this generation has a heaven without substance. Their heaven has no reality; there is nothing that the soul can really reach out and take hold of. To them heaven is an ambiguous, nebulous nothing that is reputed to follow the death of the believer — and they're supposed to really enjoy it if they ever get there."[1]

> *This book is a call to see life in the unblinking light of eternity. It is a challenge to view genuine success not in terms of earthly acclaim or possessions, but rather in terms of a "Well done" from Jesus.*

The same motivation that spurs others, the Beirut terrorists for instance, to put their earthly future on the line in lieu of eternal riches should prod Christians as well. But there is one important distinction. While the terrorists were impelled by a faulty understanding of a God of wrath, we are motivated by a biblical understanding of a God of love. "For Christ's love compels us" (2 Cor. 5:14;NIV). The prospect of eternal rewards, dispensed by Jesus himself, is the call to ultimate fulfillment. To receive Christ's approval and accompanying rewards in return for a life of service to Him — this is worth more than a million worlds.

Charles Kettering said, "We should be concerned about the future because that is where we are going to spend the rest of our lives." Yet we are probably the most immediacy-oriented Christians in history. The secularization of society has plagued the Church as well. In fact, part of the reason for the famine of preaching about heaven is that most people aren't interested. The minister wants to be relevant and preach to their felt needs. And few are feeling the need for heaven and rewards that seem roughly equivalent to celestial versions of bowling trophies.

Yet if we scratch below the surface, we find a gnawing longing for more than the material. When we are yanked out of the mad pursuit for pleasure by the death of a friend or a life-threatening accident, we realize again that we are meant for more than a daily lap in a rat race. Our sterile technology and rationalism have produced a thirst for metaphysical experience. Many attempt to quench this thirst by bizarre trips into forms of Eastern religions or flirtations with the occult. But this inner thirst can only be satiated by coming to the One who almost 2,000 years ago said, "If anyone thirsts, let him come to Me and drink" (John 7:37).

Years ago E.M. Bounds sounded a prophetic warning that has been largely fulfilled. "These are materialized and materializing times," he wrote. "Materialized times always exalt the earthly and degrade the heavenly. True Christianity always diminishes the earthly and augments the heavenly. If God's watchmen are not brave, diligent, and sleepless, Christianity will catch the contagion of the times and think little of and struggle less for heaven."[2]

Existential Christianity

It is indicative of the times that a recent edition of a major evangelical denomination's hymnal has deleted no fewer than 17 hymns dealing with heaven and eternal rewards. Among these hymns apparently considered obsolete, one heart-searching song asks,

> *Must I go, and empty-handed,*
> *Thus my dear Redeemer meet?*

Not one day of service give Him,
Lay no trophy at His feet?[3]

Hymns about the sweet by-and-by have been replaced with lusterless lyrics about the gritty present. Even the old hymns we retain are often "contemporized" versions that delete references to rewards in heaven. Note, for instance, the deletion of this stanza in almost all hymnals from the popular Christian song "Redeemed" by Fanny Crosby:

I know that there's a crown that is waiting
In yonder bright mansion for me,
And soon, with the spirits made perfect,
At home with the Lord I shall be.[4]

Honestly, I hurt for Christians who attempt to "tough it out" with no concept of eternity. Much of our teaching has become essentially courses in positive thinking with a light Bible glaze on top. How sad to view trials, pressures, temptations, and reversals from a purely temporal perspective. One may be encouraged to "hang on, better days are coming." But what if they don't come? Is faith then shipwrecked? It would be if there were no glimpse of eternity.

The facts are that things don't always add up down here. Good is not always compensated in kind. It will take another world for Christians who serve God and others in secret to be rewarded justly and openly.

Any Christianity that is devoid of an eternal perspective is a stripped-down model and should be traded in for something sturdier. Frankly, if your brand of teaching says this life is all there is, you've gotten a raw deal theologically. The Bible says, "If in this life *only* we have hope in Christ, we are of all men the most pitiable" (1 Cor. 15:19).

When this life is viewed as a mere blip on eternity's scale, the most rigorous trials can become "light afflictions" and prolonged agonies can be seen as "but for a moment."

In all probability, Paul was in the throes of personal pain, heartbreaking distress, and satanic attack when he wrote, "For our light affliction, which is but for a moment, is working for us a far more exceeding and eternal weight of glory, while we do not look at the things which are seen, but at the things which are not seen. For the things which are seen are temporary, but the things which are not seen are eternal" (2 Cor. 4:17-18).

It was with this confidence in God's ultimate rule that Alexander Solzhenitsyn was able to find solace in the most nightmarish of circumstances. Speaking of his Gulag Archipelago experience, he reminisced, "I nourished my soul there, and I say without hesitation: '*Bless you prison*, for having been in my life.' "[5]

Ironically, it becomes not the positive pep talks but the confidence of eternal blessings with Christ that breeds superlative living in the midst of storms. So trade in the current model of futureless faith for a Christianity that won't depreciate. The measure of blessing may not be "instant return" on what you have sown, but that kind of return usually evaporates anyway. Rather, you will walk joyfully by faith, banking on a tomorrow when a just God will reward justly — with no favoritism. The ministry of God's Spirit to you becomes your guarantee that even more wonderful things are ahead. We might restate Paul's words in 2 Corinthians 5:4 to say: "For we who are in these mortal bodies groan, not because we have a death wish, but because we long to be clothed with immortality, that mortality may be swallowed up by life."

A pretty good gauge of spiritual health is to be ready at any given moment to drop it all — no matter how great the earthly blessings — to be home with the Lord. In a word, it's just better. Like Paul, we recognize our responsibilities to family, friends, jobs. So we stay until He re-stations us. But we are not conned into believing that our ultimate rewards come in this life. There's something more — more permanent, more wonderful, more fulfilling. "To depart and be with Christ . . . is *far better!*" (Phil. 1:23).

So That's This Ache

Recently, I talked with a friend about writing this book. At first she seemed thoroughly disinterested. "What do I need with a book about heaven and rewards?" she asked. "I'm too caught up with getting my kids to piano lessons and helping my husband advance in his work."

But as I probed a little deeper her curiosity increased. "So *that's* this ache I've been feeling," she said. "I've had this inner longing for something, but I couldn't put my finger on it. I guess it's really a longing for heaven. I never thought about it because nobody's been suggesting that's what this longing is." And if we continue to search our souls, we discover that, behind the longing for heaven is an innate longing for God himself. As theologian Karl Barth once said, "There are two kinds of people in the world: those who have found God and those who are looking for Him."

The Bible confirms this built-in longing for eternity. "For we know that if our earthly house, this tent, is destroyed, we have a building from God, a house not made with hands, eternal in the heavens. For in this we groan, earnestly desiring to be clothed with our habitation which is from heaven" (2 Cor. 5:1-2). The very word for *man* or *human* in Greek means "upward looker." We are eternal beings. This life is merely an interim. And something inside us knows it.

I believe we are poised to see a revolt of sorts against "relevant" teaching and preaching that is largely irrelevant to our deepest longings. And the heart's deepest longing, contrary to some popular sermonizing, is not for health or wealth. Our deepest yearning is for God himself.

Bishop Leighton of London was often criticized for not preaching to the times. "While everyone is preaching to the times," he responded, "may not one poor soul speak for eternity?" I realize that this book is something of a voice crying in the wilderness. On the surface, teaching on daily struggles seems far more practical than a call to set one's affection on another world. Yet, in the dark nights of the soul (and all of us have them), we cry for a redefinition of relevancy. We look for something — anything — that *really lasts.*

Clouded Thinking About the Unclouded Day

Many have an idea of heaven that is not that far removed from Huck Finn's. He viewed heaven as a place where people "go around all day long with a harp and sing, forever and ever." But for discerning Christians, the life after this one is but the eternal continuation and intensifying of the new life we began when we trusted Christ as Lord and Saviour. On that day we were genuinely converted — not just our souls, but our values. Things previously held dear began to be unattractive, and things once disdained are now embraced. Motivation itself begins to change: no longer is our passion merely to please ourselves. Rather, we long to please Him. "Therefore we make it our aim, whether present or absent, to be well pleasing to Him" (2 Cor. 5:9). Not content to merely serve the Lord, we wish to serve Him acceptably. "Therefore, since we are receiving a kingdom which cannot be shaken, let us have grace, by which we may serve God acceptably with reverence and godly fear. For our God is a consuming fire" (Heb. 12:28-29).

The Bible teaches that Christians will one day stand before the Lord, not recoiling in fear of possible expulsion, but to receive His affirmation. There, at what the Bible terms the Judgment Seat of Christ, the Christian will be held accountable for his post-conversion life; each action and the motive behind it will be weighed. This is both sobering and exciting. No wonder Charles Spurgeon said, "We should live each moment as though it were being recorded; for recorded it shall be."

Obviously such a prospect is a powerful prod to holy living since our selfish deeds will be exposed. But it is also a joyful expectation. It is before this Judgment Seat that Jesus will reward good deeds. He will bestow honors that will outlast time for those who qualify.

It is little wonder that many Christians are confused and disillusioned today. For if we view things from the perspective of this life only, it could appear that God is playing favorites. Some, who have labored seemingly in vain, would be tempted to conclude that He is unjust, that He has forgotten His promises to relieve the downtrodden and restore the righteous.

But *if,* in fact, there is a day when cups of cold water secretly ministered in His name are openly honored, and *if* there is an event when the scales of justice are forever balanced, then the bleakest of pictures bursts with rays of hope. Surely this is at least part of what the Lord had in mind when He promised a day of radical power reversal when the meek shall inherit the earth. A.W. Tozer describes the meek person as the trusting believer who is "patient to wait for the day when everything will get its own price tag and real worth will come into its own. Then the righteous shall shine forth in the kingdom of their Father. He is willing to wait for that day."[6]

Perhaps the reason some avoid the subject of heaven is a subliminal fear of standing before God. But if indeed we belong to Him through faith in His Son, there is nothing to fear. As the old hymn declares, we will be "dressed in His righteousness alone, faultless to stand before the throne."[7] The future prospect for the person who knows Christ is always bright. What do you, as a Christian, have to look forward to in heaven? In a word, kindness. This is part of the reason why the next life is eternity-long. It will take that long for God to express the full scope of His love to you. "That in the ages to come He might show the exceeding riches of His grace in His kindness toward us in Christ Jesus" (Eph. 2:7). What a future!

One Hundred Years from Today

So life's great issue becomes one of living for what is ultimately important. What are we doing now that will be important to us 100 years from today? If we prioritize in light of that question, we find that the abiding components are amazingly few. Very quickly the list is whittled down to relationships.

One hundred years from today your present income will be inconsequential. One hundred years from now it won't matter if you got that big break, took the trip to Europe, or finally traded up to a Mercedes. The insensitive remarks about you will be long since dead as will be the people who made them. The fact that you threw pizza dough for a living or threw fits in a corporate boardroom will not matter.

It will matter that you knew God. It will greatly matter, 100 years from now, that you made a commitment to Jesus Christ. It will matter what you said since every idle word will be brought into judgment (see Matt. 12:36). It will matter what you did when you thought no one was looking since every secret thing will be exposed (see Matt. 10:26). It will be important that you loved your children (and other's children) and that you helped provide a base of emotional acceptance on which they built their lives. It will matter that you fit into God's purposes — not only His purposes for your life but His purposes for your generation.

Most of us spend a minimum of 40 hours a week investing in the present. Of course, this is both necessary and commendable. Honest labor is honorable. But all of our involvements in current happenings are just little glitches on eternity's continuum. While we spend vast amounts of time responding to the necessities of the passing present, wouldn't it be prudent also to make some kind of preparation for what is permanent?

Intersections with Eternity

We are trained to stuff the most experience possible

into the shortest time frame possible. Perhaps one reason for this is the uncertainty so many feel about the future. Teenagers, not at all sure that their planet will survive another decade, want to taste the full gamut of life "before it's too late." Hedonists preach that we should live only for today. Stores lure the already overextended with the most seductive bait — "You can have it now!" — with no worries about payments until after the first of the year. A lifetime of character development is bartered for a single night of passion. Clearly, we are a generation geared to sacrificing the eternal on the altar of the immediate.

Yet life's transcendent experiences beckon us back to ultimate realities. To be present at the birth of a child is to experience a miracle — the miracle of life. But even in this joyous celebration there's a little prick on the conscience, a reminder that this baby has not only begun to live, this child has also begun to die.

Birth and death are transcendent experiences, times when earth touches eternity. But there is another birth, just as real, in some ways more real than physical birth. It is the new birth Jesus spoke of so often. And unless one experiences this birth, he or she cannot experience true life here or hereafter. It is a trip back to ultimate roots, for one reverses the process of physical growth to be born again spiritually. He moves back to a childlike dependency on God alone ("becoming as a little child") so that he can then be reborn. Placing himself fully in the hands of God, turning absolutely from any self-reliance, he trusts the sacrifice of the One who died in his place. And he enters a realm of transcendent spiritual reality previously unknown.

Have you experienced this new birth? Heaven is indeed a cruel joke unless you come to know and love the Lord who reigns there. Perhaps some deep longing is being evoked in you even now, as you read. An inner thirst, long suppressed, is suddenly screaming for living water.

Your thirst can be quenched. Your life can intersect

eternity — starting now. And listen to this promise from the One who dispenses this water: "Whoever drinks of the water that I shall give him will never thirst. But the water that I shall give him will become in him a fountain of water springing up into everlasting life" (John 4:14).

Do you want this water? Do you desire this new birth? Then open your heart to Jesus Christ right now. Let Him pour His living water over your parched soul. Make this the prayer of your heart.

> *Lord Jesus, I want this living water. I want to be born again, on the inside. Thank You for dying on the cross for me. Right now, I repent of my sins and trust Your shed blood as full payment for all my sins. I believe that You are the Son of God and that God has raised You from the dead. I now receive You as my personal Saviour and commit myself unreservedly to You as Lord. Thank You for hearing my prayer, forgiving my sins, and coming into my life as You promised.*

Did you sincerely pray that prayer? Then, welcome to God's worldwide family. Welcome to a new realm in which life intersects with eternity. You now belong to God: "But as many as received Him, to them He gave the right to become children of God, even to those who believe in His name" (John 1:12).

The Christian's life is an adventure of knowing God, walking with God, and living in the light of eternity. And at the end of life on this earth, the Christian can stand before Christ and learn what ultimate success really means.

2

An Abundant Entrance

Therefore, brethren, be even more diligent to make your call and election sure, for if you do these things you will never stumble; for so an entrance will be supplied to you abundantly into the everlasting kingdom of our Lord and Savior Jesus Christ (2 Pet. 1:10-11).

Several years ago I met a young British pastor. Since we lived on opposites sides of the Atlantic we seldom saw each other, but we maintained contact through correspondence. I was saddened to hear some time back that he fought a losing battle with cancer. He carried on his ministry in wrenching pain and exhaustion. But his love for Christ and his people helped pump spiritual adrenaline into his weakening body.

He wrote me concerning a series of messages he was preaching. Not surprisingly, the subject was heaven. He wrote: "I've preached a timely series on Christian behavior concluding with 2 Peter 1:11, 'an abundant entrance into heaven.' I believe we can enter heaven in different manners (though the sole way in is through Christ). So few seem to want this abundant entrance. Like Balaam, they wish to die the death of the righteous but are not prepared to live the life of the righteous (2 Pet. 2:15)."

When one is faced with the acute prospect of stepping into eternity, heaven (and hell) appear more tangible. Indeed, the afterlife becomes as real (or more real) than this ephemeral stage. Shakespeare said, somewhat pessimistically, "All the world's a stage, and all the men and women merely players."[1] It is true that we are living out a drama that will be judged in the next world.

While many of today's televangelists primarily emphasize the blessings of God in the present, it was not always so. A handful of decades ago, in the early 1940s, things were quite different. The big-name evangelist of the time was Charles E. Fuller and his "Old-Fashioned Revival Hour" was broadcast live to millions worldwide on Sunday afternoons from the Municipal Auditorium in Long Beach. The audience filling the auditorium was often composed of sailors awaiting orders to be sent to the watery battlefronts of the Pacific.

Fuller realized that for many of these young men, each broadcast could be their last chance to hear the gospel and respond to Jesus Christ. His immense compassion reached out to those sailors and they committed their lives to Christ by the hundreds.

By the radio sets back home anxious parents sat listening, praying that their sons were in attendance. And many grieving parents and newly widowed young women were listening who had only recently heard the life-altering news of the deaths of their loved ones in battle. Dr. Fuller was sensitive to the needs of the multitudes who were staring death in the face. Along with his messages about eternity, he instructed his music director to include in every broadcast no fewer than three songs about heaven.

Death is just as stark now as it was then. Could it be that what grieving millions need to hear is not just a pep talk to be strong, but a message of assurance that, for the Christian, there is a better life after this one?

This Year's Model or Historic Faith?

Why does heaven seem to have no allure for most of us? Philip Yancey, in an excellent article, "Heaven Can't Wait,"[2] suggests several reasons. One, he explains, is that many Americans are affluent enough to buy whatever they want; earlier generations looked to heaven for this abundance of luxuries. During the Depression of the 1930s, for instance, many escaped to the movies to live vicariously in southern mansions or New York penthouses. Others faced this life squarely in hopes of a better life to come.

The decades have taken the edge off acute hunger and poverty for many Americans. Reinforced by an advertising assault that assures us that we can have heaven on earth (provided we have the right products), many simply don't want to opt for a heaven they haven't seen when they *have* seen Beverly Hills.

A further result of our ability to consume in this life is that the "older images of heaven, the biblical ones, have lost their appeal." Streets paved with gold may not be the most practical surface for Porsches. And an endless praise and worship service doesn't seem quite as appealing to many as a good concert or movie.

How tragically ironic that, while our generation forgoes the prospects for mansions of unspeakable splendor that will never devalue or deteriorate, we stay up late to lust after the homes and the lifestyles of the rich and famous.

Yancey also suggests that many are indifferent to the afterlife because "a creeping paganism" convinces us that death is the end of life. The more our faith is enmeshed with materialism, the more it is akin to paganism. We hear 50 sermons on "How You Can Get What You Want from God" to every one message we hear on "How God Can Get What He Wants from You."

> *Incredibly, the more rapidly we race toward the latter days and judgment, the less we are exhorted to "Prepare to meet your God."*

Even among some Bible-believing Christians, there seems to be some question as to the reality of judgment. Yet neither Scripture nor our historic posture on the subject leaves any doubt as to the final destiny of those without Christ.

Scripture clearly describes a coming Apocalypse ". . . when the Lord Jesus is revealed from heaven with His mighty angels, in flaming fire taking vengeance on those who do not know God, and on those who do not obey the gospel of the Lord Jesus Christ. These shall be punished with everlasting destruction from the presence of the Lord and from the glory of His power" (2 Thess. 1:7-9).

Polycarp, one of the Early Church fathers, faced a vicious martyrdom in a Roman arena with wild beasts. The proconsul urged this aged Christian to renounce his faith in Christ but to no avail. Finally he threatened, "I will have you consumed with fire, if you despise wild beasts, unless you change your mind." Polycarp replied, "You threaten fire which burns for an hour and is soon quenched; for you are ignorant of the fire of the coming judgment and eternal punishment reserved for the wicked." Polycarp, having already given himself up for dead, sought only the salvation of his executioner.[3]

To the testimony of Scripture and countless Christian martyrs, the historic creeds of Christendom add their affirmation of a real heaven and a real hell. One of the great theological documents of history is the Westminster Confession. This statement of faith declares clearly, ". . . But the wicked, who know not God, and obey not the gospel of Jesus

Christ, shall be cast into eternal torments, and be punished with everlasting destruction from the presence of the Lord, and from the glory of His power."

In more modern times as well evangelical Christians have affirmed the reality not only of a place of eternal blessing, but also a place of eternal torment. The Baptist Faith and Message states, "The unrighteous will be consigned to hell, the place of everlasting punishment. The righteous in their resurrected and glorified bodies will receive their reward and will dwell forever in Heaven with the Lord." The Statement of Fundamental Truths of the Assemblies of God declares, "Whosoever is not found written in the Book of Life, together with the devil and his angels, the beast and the false prophet, will be consigned to everlasting punishment in the lake which burneth with fire and brimstone, which is the second death."

It is not that we have formally removed our belief in heaven and hell. It is simply that there is an eerie silence, even among evangelicals, as many endeavor to sort out in their heart of hearts what they really hold to be true.

The Secret of Living Forever

Comedian George Burns quipped, "The secret of living forever is to live to be 100 — because very few people die after they're 100!"

We don't like to think that death is an appointed experience for humanity. We want to avoid death — to live forever. Actually, the secret of living forever is not to avoid death but to prepare for it. And the proper preparation is by no means morbid. In fact, to be properly prepared to die launches us into a life of freedom and joy.

If we would know the secret of living forever we must ask what constitutes eternal life. And Jesus (the One who is really an authority on living forever) gives us the answer. "And this is eternal life," He prayed to His Father, "that they may know You, the only true God, and Jesus Christ whom You have sent" (John 17:3). To know Jesus Christ is to be steeped in life — abundant and eternal life.

One night evangelist Billy Sunday found himself in a seedy section of Chicago confronted by myriad vices. Turning compassionately to a group involved in degrading actions, he said, "Men, why don't you live the way you know you want to die?" We are prepared to live only if we are prepared to die. Thus prepared, the Christian not only anticipates meeting God in heaven, his earthly life teems with experiences in which he is meeting God at every turn.

One early Christian bishop offered this succinct eulogy of Christians thrown to lions for sport: "Our people die well." To live well is to know God and Jesus Christ whom He has sent — not just in a superficial fashion but in an ever deepening love-commitment.

A Rich Welcome

There's an abundant entrance into heaven for those who live well. Simply put, living well is living for Jesus. When He returns — as surely He will — how will you greet Him? He may come for you at the hour of your death. Or you may be alive to welcome His return to earth. In either case, He's coming for you. Are you ready to meet Him?

Not all Christians will greet the Lord in the same way. John warned, "And now, little children, abide in Him, that when He appears, we may have confidence and not be ashamed before Him at His coming" (1 John 2:28). Some parts of His blushing Bride will be blushing for the wrong reasons. Let me give you an example.

The most wonderful blessing in my life other than Jesus is Naomi, my wife. Because of the nature of the ministry in my trust, I am sometimes away from my family for weeks at a time, often on the other side of the world. But, as with the description of the virtuous woman in Proverbs, "the heart of her husband safely trusts her" (Prov. 31:11).

Some men who travel frequently are not so fortunate. If a husband were to return after a long trip, only to find his wife strangely evasive and "ashamed before him" he would have reason to suspect unfaithfulness. With the bride of Christ as well, those who blush at Christ's return are the spiritually unfaithful. They have had affairs of the heart, loving the world and the things that are in the world. Some Christians will not welcome the Lord with open face, but rather they will hide their faces from Him.

Or to continue the illustration, suppose a returning husband got this reception: Haggard and distressed, his wife exclaims, "Boy, am I glad to see you! Everything's a mess. The house is a wreck. I haven't had time to do any of those things you wanted me to do. I'm so glad you're back. I need a permanent vacation. You take over!"

How do you think the husband would take such a "welcome"? Yet many Christians anticipate Christ's return as an escape from pressure. Not about the Master's business, their frazzled lives are a jumbled mess of "urgent" involvements, while they consistently put concerns of timeless importance on the back burner.

Or suppose a returning husband were to discover his wife had been completely nonproductive while he was away. "I just waited for you to come back and take care of things. After all, you're so much better at everything than I am. I thought my best course of action was just to stay out of the way and watch soap operas until you got here." This rocking-chair mentality has infected many believers. Jesus even told a story about such poor stewardship. He compared some workers for the Kingdom to the one who buried his talent in the ground to be sure to protect it. Scripture records that the Lord was angry with that slothful servant.

Now back to Naomi. When I come from a time away, the house is always clean and in order. Our sons have obviously been well cared for. "Have you been able to get those items for me?" I ask.

"Of course, honey," she says.

No wonder I love coming home!

Come, Lord Jesus

What kind of Bride do you think Jesus loves coming home to? No doubt the one who has done what He left for her to do. And He left us a Great Commission to go disciple the nations to Him. We dare not occupy our lives with anything else (even good things) except the one clear thing He left for us to do.

You are of infinite worth to God and to His plan for your generation. So don't slowly drown your life in trivia. Oswald Chambers said, "One's individual life may be of priceless value to God's purposes, and yours may be that life."[4] God's purposes in any generation are fulfilled by people, people who are poised to hear and obey His agenda for their times. Our day is no different. We cannot allow ourselves to be drugged into indifference. The challenge to believers today is to rip ourselves away from the trivia trap and sensitize ourselves to heaven's directives.

I've often looked at the unprecedented challenges the Church faces today and asked, "God, where are the Moodys? Where are the Wesleys?" His reply back to my heart, amazing as it seems, is, "I chose them for their day. I have chosen you for yours." *You* have been chosen for this era, and there's never been a time like this. Imagine how much God trusts you to entrust the bearing of His name in this generation to you.

Not only that; think of what you have seen, and will yet see, that godly men and women of the past longed to see but never saw. "For assuredly, I say to you that many prophets and righteous men desired to see what you see, and did not see it, and to hear what you hear, and did not hear it" (Matt. 13:17). Without question, "You are a chosen generation, a royal priesthood, a holy nation, His own special people, that you may proclaim the praises of Him who called you out of darkness into His marvelous light" (1 Pet. 2:9).

Samuel Johnson, commenting on a man who was expecting to be hanged, said, "The prospect of death wonderfully concentrates the mind."[5] So, without any macabre obsession with death, prepare to meet your God. And by doing so, prepare for a life of uncluttered joy — for the priorities in such a life are clear and few. It boils down to pleasing Jesus, just living in light of His coming.

In seminary I took a course in evangelism under an extraordinary professor, Dr. Oscar Thompson, during the last semester he was able to teach. This man of immense faith was dying of cancer.

I remember the simplicity and joy with which he taught. Limping into class and leaning heavily on his cane, he was a beautiful mixture of desiring to compress as much life as possible into a short amount of time and a holy nonchalance about temporal things. One thing Dr. Thompson said which I will never forget: "God doesn't give grace on non-dying days." Until his last breath, he had a fragrant grace for living. Then, on Promotion Day, not only did he receive dying grace, he received an abundant entrance.

3

For Time and Eternity

For he was looking forward to the city with foundations, whose architect and builder is God (Heb. 11:10;NIV).

It's difficult to conceive of heaven since all our experience is earthbound and timebound. And because all our experiences involve us directly, it becomes quite a challenge to imagine a place where God is central, not man. But there is indeed such a place. In fact, a slice of heaven is transplanted in us when we crown Jesus as Lord of our lives. For then, although imperfectly, we come under the same reign as heaven. Our existence is no longer measured by time: we have embarked on eternal life. Let's see if we can get a clear picture of heaven.

A Glimpse of Eternity

Many people claim to have had a glimpse of heaven and are beginning to feel freer to describe their out-of-body experiences. For a culture baptized in rationalism, both Christians and non-Christians often tend to take such stories with at least a pretty good-sized grain of salt. But now the evidence is mounting and one particular pattern seems to be emerging. At the outset most speak of an overpowering light and an irresistible attraction to that light, whatever (or whoever) it is.

It is puzzling to some Christians that those who claim no allegiance to Jesus Christ also speak of this "light" coming for them at the point of death. This should not be puzzling if we remember Satan's angelic title was Lucifer, Star of the Morning. Ever since his mutiny, he retains remarkable powers of figure transformation: "For Satan himself transforms himself into an angel of light" (2 Cor. 11:14). We know he appeared as a beautiful serpent in the Garden. It should be no surprise that he can appear as a beautiful light coming to claim his own. In both cases, his scheme is deception. As the serpent, he deceived Eve. As the "light," he can deceive those in the process of dying, who have never committed themselves to Christ, that everything is fine. The Bible warns against this beautiful, yet eternally deadly chameleon quality of the devil.

Having given this caution, I must hasten to say that I believe many out-of-body experiences are genuine samplings of heaven. The experiences of many dying Christians lend comfort to those left behind. Betty Malz describes her experience after being declared clinically dead (and later being revived) in her book, *My Glimpse of Eternity.*

> [The angel and I] came upon a magnificent silver structure. It was like a palace except there were no towers. As we walked toward it, I heard voices. They were melodious, harmonious, blending in chorus and I heard the word "Jesus." There were more than four parts to their harmony. I not only heard the singing and felt the singing but I joined the singing. I have always had a girl's body, but a low boy's voice. Suddenly I

realized I was singing the way I had always wanted to . . . in high, clear and sweet tones.

After a while the music softened, then the unseen voices picked up a new chorus. The voices not only burst forth in more than four parts, but they were in different languages. I was awed by the richness and perfect blending of the words — and I could understand them! I do not know why this was possible except that I was part of a universal experience.

While the angel and I walked together I sensed we could go wherever we willed ourselves to go and be there instantly. Communication between us was through the projection of thoughts. The words sung in all the different languages were understandable, but I don't know how or why. We all seemed to be on some universal wavelength.

I thought at the time, "I will never forget the melody and these words." But later I could only recall two: "Jesus" and "redeemed."

The angel stepped forward and put the palm of his hand upon a gate which I had not noticed before. About twelve feet high, the gate was a solid sheet of pearl, with no handles and some lovely scroll work at the top of its Gothic structure. The pearl was translucent so that I could almost, but not quite, see inside. The atmosphere inside was somehow filtered through. My feeling was of ecstatic joy and anticipation at the thought of going inside.

When the angel stepped forward, pressing his palm on the gate, an opening appeared in the center of the pearl panel and slowly widened and deepened as though the translucent material was dissolving. Inside I saw what appeared to be a street of golden color with an overlay of glass or water. The yellow light that appeared was dazzling. There is no way to describe it. I saw no figure, yet I was conscious of a Person. Suddenly I knew that the light was Jesus, the Person was Jesus.

I did not have to move. The light was all about me. There seemed to be some heat in it as if I were standing in sunlight; my body began to glow. Every part of me was absorbing the light. I felt bathed by the rays of a powerful, penetrating, loving energy.[1]

Betty's experience coincides with John's revelation of this eternal, magnificent city. "And the city had no need of the sun or of the moon to shine in it, for the glory of God illuminated it, and the Lamb is its light . . . And there shall be no night there: They need no lamp nor light of the sun, for the Lord God gives them light" (Rev. 21:23; 22:5).

In describing part of God's character, the Bible says, "God is light and in Him is no darkness at all" (1 John 1:5). Since this heavenly city is God's abode, it follows that there is no night; there is only constant light and, therefore, constant revelation and illumination. What a conducive climate for growth!

Blueprint of Heaven

R.G. Lee was one of the last of the great southern orator-preachers. His command of the English language was, perhaps, unexcelled by his contemporaries. I had the high privilege of hearing Dr. Lee, then in his eighties, preach on heaven at the Moody Memorial Church in Chicago. I've never heard anything like it before or since. He said with grace and eloquence what I've struggled through several drafts to say in this book. But when Dr. Lee lay on his deathbed, even this master pulpiteer was at a loss for words. He would weave in and out of consciousness with looks of rapture on his aged face. Intermittently he would say, "Oh, look. Look!" Returning briefly to consciousness, he told his nurse, "I wanted so badly to help people see heaven when I preached. But, oh, I never did it justice."

So we must see even biblical descriptions of heaven, though true, as mere accommodations to our limited ability to grasp its beauty. But let's stretch our hearts and minds and let God's Word describe something of the scope of this city.[2] According to Scripture, this heavenly city is a cube, 12,000 furlongs in length, breadth, and height. A furlong is 582-1/2 feet, or approximately one-eighth of a mile. So the dimensions of the city are 1,500 miles in all directions. If this city were set on the earth, on United States territory, it would extend from the northernmost tip of Maine to the southernmost point of Florida, and would reach from the Atlantic Ocean to the Colorado River. If it were placed over Europe it would cover all of England, France, Germany, Italy, the Eastern European countries, and half of Russia. The surface level of this New Jerusalem is a staggering 2,250,000 square miles.

But that is only the measurement of the first level! The Bible says that the city is as high as it is wide. It is not a square but a cube. Can you conceive of a building 1,500 miles tall? But this is not a building; it's an entire city built layer upon layer, mile after mile, to this incredible height.

We are specifically told that there are streets in this city, so let's assume that they are laid out on a square grid at one mile intervals. This would be far less frequent than any city on earth. This grid would give us 3,000 streets per level, each one 1,500 miles long for a total street length of 4.5 million miles per level. If we assume each level will be one mile above the preceding one, there could be as many as

1,500 of these levels, thereby giving the city over 6.7 billion miles of roads — all paved with pure gold!

The jasper walls surrounding the first level are one half-mile high. This is higher than any church spire in the world. The gates themselves are solid pearls. The city contains three and one-third billion cubic miles. Even if half of this area were allowed for streets, it would still leave room for nine quadrillion rooms 30 feet long, 30 feet wide, and 30 feet high.

Businesses are now discovering the concept that "big offices help produce big ideas." What kinds of thoughts and ideas could flow from the kind of space we've been describing!

Something to Occupy Your Time

No doubt the God of design and economy has clear uses for the vast expanses of this heavenly city. Surely the same Lord who had His disciples gather up the 12 baskets of food fragments "so that nothing will be wasted" does not wish for these massive amounts of space to go unoccupied. So what are these "cubicles" to be filled with? Redeemed people and fantastic ideas. And Scripture teaches that there will be a new earth in which these ideas can be implemented. Noble men and women have gone to their graves groping for answers to puzzling predicaments. For those who die in Christ, the process of thinking continues — but with none of the limitations of earth.

Far from being a place to recline on a cloud playing endless stanzas of "elevator music" on a harp, heaven is a place of inexpressible creativity and joy. We are most joyful and fulfilled when we are productive. As C.S. Lewis said, "Joy is the serious business of heaven."

We will continue to develop, learn, and serve, since servanthood, motivated by love, is the normal standard of conduct in this new scheme of things. In Aldous Huxley's *Brave New World*, torture and inhumane actions were the norm. But in this truly brave, redeemed world order, love motivates unselfish service.

Imagine a place of architectural perfection where all the stops are pulled out on creativity. Joseph Bayly, now living in heaven, described a fictitious (or is it?) scene in which he would ask the Lord for assistance in being acclimated to this new love-environment.

> "This work You mentioned earlier. Will it just be managing Your universe?"
>
> "Of course not. You can also plant a garden — without sweat or drought or weeds. Like Eden. You can create a poem or an oratorio. You can carve wood or paint a landscape."
>
> "To praise You."
>
> "Everything in heaven is to My praise. My people intend it so. I accept it, but that doesn't mean they only sing My praise — their work is praise to Me."
>
> "Will I be able to sing? I always wanted to."
>
> "Handel's choir always has room for one more. But, for that matter, you may want to have your own choir, to learn to conduct it — or an orchestra."[3]

Then there is the concept of a timeless eternity: an infinity of "time" (or more precisely the lack of it) in which to experiment with God's ongoing creation and to explore the depths of His character. Bound as we are to time, it is perhaps impossible even to begin to perceive an existence out of the realms of time. Scientists, however, are beginning to probe this possibility — just a little. While the idea of literal time travel is still viewed as highly improbable, Einstein has taught us that time is not fixed; it is relative. Thus we speak now of "time warps" and "freeze frames."

David Watson, a popular British writer who is now enjoying heaven, reminds us, "Time is relative to motion, as Einstein has shown us. For example, at the speed of light the passage of time vanishes. Everything happens now! Subject as we are to the dimensions of time during this life, the concept of a timeless eternity is hard, if not impossible, to grasp. We can therefore only grope for metaphors and pictures about heaven."[4]

"But," some will protest, "you can be so heavenly minded you're no earthly good." This refers to the notion that Christians might expend such energy concentrating on heaven that they fail in their responsibilities here on earth. Frankly, I've never met anyone like that. In fact, I think just the opposite happens.

Heavenly minded people seldom retreat to ivory towers. Rather, it is usually the heavenly minded who are most ready to roll up their sleeves and get to work on the problems of earth.

Look, for instance, at Mother Teresa and Mark Buntain — two "heavenly minded" sojourners who gave their lives for the diseased and impoverished of Calcutta. Remember a "heavenly minded" Wilberforce whose passion for human dignity helped eradicate the slave trade throughout the British empire. Go to the inner city of Chicago and watch the tireless workers at the Pacific Garden Mission as they tell inquiring street people how to get to heaven while providing them food and shelter on the way. Scan the world and look at the thousands of hospitals, shelters, leprosariums, children's homes, and colleges that have been built in heaven's honor. The point is obvious. Those who truly set their sights on another world are often the most active for constructive change in this one.

C.S. Lewis said, "The Apostles themselves, who set on foot the conversion of the Roman Empire, the great men who built up the Middle Ages, the English Evangelicals who abolished the Slave Trade, all left their mark on Earth, precisely because their minds were occupied with Heaven.

It is since Christians have largely ceased to think of the other world that they have become so ineffective in this one."[5]

Heaven on Earth

The Bible says that "here we have no continuing city, but we seek the one to come" (Heb. 13:14). Indeed, nothing here is permanent. Think back on your high school graduation. Remember signing the yearbooks and the promising always to stay in touch. Did they? Did you? We have no continuing city. In a 10-year span, most of the key players in your life (except your family) will probably change. And, tragically, for many the key players of family itself change.

The transient nature of life is a powerful incentive to live for eternity. But this does not nullify our responsibilities on this planet. The Christian holds his desire for another world with his stewardship in this world in tandem. Calvin Miller was right when he said, "We are living in honor of the next world while keeping our arms embraced around this one."

God's Word is clear that we are currently engaged in a cooperative effort with Him in the establishment of His purposes in the earth. While I claim no rare insights into eschatology, I do not believe Jesus was speaking tongue-in-cheek when He taught us to pray, "Your kingdom come. Your will be done *on earth* as it is in heaven" (Matt. 6:10). Surely He meant for us to pray in faith for results we could see, not only in a coming Kingdom, but also in our lifetimes.

Heaven has already established countless beachheads on earth. Each time someone receives Jesus as Lord of his or her life, a beachhead for the kingdom of God is established. At its essence, the kingdom of God is simply the unrivaled rule of God. Not only is His kingdom coming, it has already come in hearts all over the world.

Augustine spoke of this dual citizenship of Christians in his immortal treatise, *City of God.* He said that Christians indeed had a responsibility to earthly authorities but that their higher loyalty was to Jesus Christ. Whenever the two cities, the temporal city of man and the eternal city of God, collide in a conflict of values or power, the Christian is always to align with the eternal.[6]

The Celestial City

> *Heaven is more solid than earth's matter, more sure for the Christian than tomorrow's sunrise. It is a place where wounds are healed forever, hearts mended permanently, hopes realized eternally.*

"And God will wipe away every tear from their eyes; there shall be no more death, nor sorrow, nor crying; and there shall be no more pain, for the former things have passed away" (Rev. 21:4).

Passed away! On this earth when we say someone has "passed away," we are endeavoring to soften the thud of death's reality. But in heaven it is death itself that has passed away and, with death's demise, all of earth's attending sorrows.

Commenting on the fact of heaven, Edith Schaeffer said, "This is reality. Heaven is a place. There is a city we are going to see and walk in. Neither the place, nor the singing instead of the sighing, nor the pleasure instead of the pain, is an illusion. We await that which is *real*."[7]

I wonder if there is not a skeptic who is doubting as she reads, or a seeker who is hoping against hope that it may be true. Let me assure you that it is true. If it were false, there could be no true Christianity. Indeed, this is a great part of the reason for biblical Christianity's collapse in liberal circles; for a Christianity without eternity is a Christianity with the life ripped out. Then "faith" is no longer a faith; it is merely one of dozens of competing moralistic philosophies.

C.S. Lewis stated bluntly, "We are very shy nowadays of even mentioning heaven. We are afraid of the jeer about 'pie in the sky,' and of being told that we are trying to 'escape' from the duty of making a happy world here and now into the dreams of a happy world elsewhere. But either there is 'pie in the sky' or there is not. If there is not, then Christianity is false, for this doctrine is woven into its whole fabric. If there is, then this truth, like any other, must be faced . . . ."[8]

Have you faced this truth? Are you living in the joy and anticipation of this truth? Preparation for heaven begins now. And, yes, the key component is faith; faith in the sacrifice of Jesus on the cross for your sins. When you actually believe that He took *your* place, dying the death you deserved, and when you open your life to His loving control, heaven will open its doors to you. You have a sure hope.

4

The Purpose of Prosperity

If riches increase, do not set your heart on them (Ps. 62:10).

Jim was everyone's all-American success story in my high school. He seemed to have everything a guy could want. He drove a silver Corvette Stingray to school, unless he felt like riding his Harley. Handsome and likable, he was an all-star back on our football team, which went to the state playoffs. Colleges across the country were clamoring to lure him with scholarships since he was a diligent student as well. He could have dated almost any girl he wanted. Of course, he chose one of the prettiest cheerleaders.

Jim sat next to me in accounting class. One day before class I had the opportunity to share my faith in Christ with him. The bell rang, cutting me short. "Come on over tonight," he told me. "I want to hear more."

That evening I drove to his home in an affluent area of Tulsa. Frankly, I was a little intimidated as I parked my mom's Ford Falcon in back of his Corvette. Jim answered the doorbell and, as usual, he was warm, even to guys like me who weren't part of the "in crowd."

For the next hour I talked with Jim about the difference a commitment to Jesus Christ could make in his life. I urged him to receive Jesus as his Lord and Saviour.

It's branded in my memory, though it was a quarter century ago, how intensely he listened. Finally he took a deep breath and responded. "David, I'm really glad it works for you," he began. "But, man, look at what I've got. Look at who I am. I'm on a social merry-go-round and I don't have time to get off this ride and think about anything else. Thanks anyway, David, but I really don't want to hear any more about this Jesus stuff."

That was in the spring. A few months later I was standing in line at a hamburger stand when another friend hit me with the news. "Did you hear about Jim?" he asked.

"Only that he's getting ready to go to college on a football scholarship," I said.

"Well, they found him yesterday in a field. He put a rifle in his mouth and blew his brains out."

Jim's tragedy is one more statistical affirmation that life does not consist in the abundance of things a person possesses. I've driven past the stores on Rodeo Drive in Beverly Hills. I've also been in the crowded, garbage-heap slums of Mexico City. I discovered one commonality in both environments: desperate people.

Poverty is an insult to the dignity of persons. But the proclivity toward sophisticated idolatry among the rich is equally dehumanizing. And part of our disinterest in an eternal heaven is because of our attempt to substitute a temporal heaven here. Judson Cornwall said, "So the saints of all ages have anticipated heaven as a city — except the people of this generation, whose application of most of the Scriptures is very materialistic and humanistic, until they begin to think of heaven. Then they try to make exclusive spiritual application of what seems to be so clearly stated as a literal place — a city for heaven's residents to dwell in."[1]

Success By Whose Definition?

What, then, constitutes true prosperity or true success? One thing I know: We are all influenced by our environment. "Success" has different definitions for different social groups. To escape the ghetto and get a high school education is success for the young person who is born there. But success may also be for a wealthy college graduate to leave suburbia to live, work, and serve in the slums.

Perhaps few words are more polarizing among Christians today than the word *prosperity.* To some, prosperity means pretentious flaunting of money. To others, prosperity means being personally secure with resources left to give to others. I lean toward the latter understanding. And, using this definition, Scripture has nothing against prosperity. Indeed, even a cursory reading of books like the Proverbs indicates that stewardship is godly and usually produces wealth — a gain that is spiritual and financial.

The problem is, we tend to go overboard on the financial side. Instead of accepting money as a means of sharing with others, we measure success by how much we can make. Yet Jesus clearly proclaimed life's highest successes to be spiritual. To be rightly related to God and people — this is true success. Material success is often a mocking deceiver; how many millions of Jims are there who financially, athletically, or academically blow the top off the scales, then one day blow their brains out?

Even the likes of Joseph Stalin spoke of the "dizziness of success." Indeed, the deadly mixture of wealth and ease can quickly hallucinate one's perception of what is real. James Matthew Barrie noted incisively in his novel *The Twelve-Pound Book,* "One's religion is whatever he is most interested in, and yours is Success."[2] If this is true, then money and success are not America's pastime, they are its passionately-held religion.

The success syndrome has infested much of the Church. On this tenuous theology/philosophy that success is measured primarily by what we can see or touch, we have mortgaged our hopes well into the next century and weighed down our present opportunities with an albatross of debt.

It should be noted, however, that simplicity does not equal puniness and ineptness. All of us know Christians who have taken holiness to the point of sterility and simplicity to the point of inverted pride. We can be simple without being simplistic. Evangelistic advance takes money. Mission endeavors take money. And even in ministries to the poor, somebody's got to buy the soup. We know that in Jesus' own ministry on earth He and the disciples were supported in part by others. Luke tells us that certain women who had been "healed of evil spirits and infirmities . . . provided for Him from their substance" (Luke 8:2-3).

Some would say money itself is amoral. Its qualities are intrinsically neither good nor evil. It is the use of money that spoils it and makes it "filthy lucre." But we also must admit that money often spoils people. We have all seen the very public changes in preachers, politicians, and businessmen whose integrity seemed impeccable *until* they had a wad of discretionary cash. Yet a thirst for success seems inbred in all of us. Is this inordinate? Hardly. God himself has put a desire in people to achieve their potential. Yet admittedly few, if any, ever reach their entire potential. Some may come close in certain areas (for example, a gymnast who performs a routine to perfection), but the perfection does not spill over into all other areas of life.

Why, then, has the Church so often spoken only in terms of success? Life is not one unbroken string of successes. Rather, it is a mix of strivings and failings, wins and losses. As Robert Browning wrote,

> *Fail I alone, in words and deeds?*
> *Why, all men strive, and who succeeds?*[3]

Neither success nor failure is permanent. If you're on

a down cycle right now, be reminded of that. And, if you're currently in a "success mode," remember it, too. Don't become intoxicated by success. Intoxication distorts reality.

You Can't Take It with You

Paul reminds us what constitutes true gain in life. "But godliness with contentment is great gain" (1 Tim. 6:6). By that definition, I've seen missionaries who voluntarily sacrificed first world splendor for Third World squalor, with great gain. I've witnessed godly grandmothers in low-income housing with great gain. I've seen the economically destitute with great gain.

This does not mean that we have no moral responsibility to the poor to help them out of their economic plight. On the contrary, we are enjoined as Christians to help lift people out of every debilitation. Certainly, to be economically disadvantaged is to be debilitated in helping others. We must understand, however, that the prayers of a godly ghetto-dweller are often of far greater value than the financial aid of a wealthy philanthropist.

Jesus reminded His disciples, "But he who is greatest among you shall be your servant. And whoever exalts himself will be abased, and he who humbles himself will be exalted" (Matt. 23:11-12). The principles set forth in these verses do indeed have validity for this life. But, if we're honest, we must admit that such a lifestyle does not always have an immediate payoff. For the truth is that servants are not always exalted; sometimes they faithfully serve insensitive masters. And those who humble themselves are sometimes not promoted but overlooked. Once again, however, we need to be reminded that this brief time frame is only a small portion of a never-ending life. The principle *does* work although the fulfillment may be in another world.

The same is true regarding giving of finances. Giving to God always produces a return: "Give, and it will be given to you" (Luke 6:38). The full returns may not be immediate or even in our lifetime. And it is precisely this point that many "faith" preachers are failing to tell their hearers. Yes, there is reward in this life for obedience to scriptural principles of giving. But many thousands of frustrated believers wonder what went wrong when they gave and, seemingly, nothing happened. The exhortation to "hang on" was appreciated. Yet, somehow, they know there were other dynamics at work, some missing components they had failed to grasp. To be told that their faith was deficient was simply adding insult to injury.

For, you see, many of the "financial counselors" are misleading people into thinking they are investing for a quick return when, in fact, they may be laying up treasures in heaven. Everybody would like to know how to double his money in less than 30 days. And sometimes we seem to think that $50 in the offering plate today will invariably yield $100 by the end of the month. But this is just not always true and even to imply it is a serious breach of trust between the spiritual investment counselor and the hopeful contributor.

When we give, we release our money to the Lord. And, of course, we release it in faith — not faith in the investment, faith in the Lord. It is God himself who has promised to supply all our needs (Phil. 4:19). Out of His own bounty entrusted to us, we give back to Him in faith that our stewardship will be deemed worthy of His further blessings.

A sure antidote to greed is to wrap the heart around the purposes of God. And the first step in doing that is to divest substantial personal treasure into God's work. Jesus taught that our heart follows our treasure, not *vice versa*. We are prone to think that giving follows commitment of heart to a vision. Not so, says the Lord: "Where your treasure is, there will your heart be also" (Matt. 6:21). Our hearts obediently follow our giving.

The pseudo-gospel of greed has infested a good portion of conservative Christianity. It is no coincidence that this message flourished in a climate of affluence among evangelicals. Theology is invariably influenced by time and culture. But we are turning an important economic corner. The United States has slipped from its position as the world's greatest creditor into the slot of the world's largest debtor. Now watch. Our theology will eventually catch up to the new economic reality. There will be a balancing of the prosperity message. In fact, it has already begun.

But the point is, in any economic climate, servanthood is always the Christian standard. Faithful, systematic giving and prudent stewardship is in order whether our income is $10,000 or $100,000. And the implication that "gain is godliness" is always a distortion of biblical truth. Paul warned Timothy to steer clear of those who taught this. Contentment was always to be prized over wealth. Those who taught otherwise were, according to Paul, "men of corrupt minds and destitute of the truth . . . For the love of money is a root of all kinds of evil, for which some have strayed from the faith in their greediness, and pierced themselves through with many sorrows. But you, O man of God, flee these things and pursue righteousness, godliness, faith, love, patience, gentleness" (1 Tim. 6:5, 10-11).

That is the message the New Testament and *that* posture of life yields dividends here and hereafter.

The Gospel to the Poor

It is worth noting that Jesus was born among the poor and His anointing for ministry was to the poor. He sensed personal fulfillment of Isaiah's prophecy when He announced, "The Spirit of the Lord is upon Me, because He has anointed Me to preach the gospel to the poor" (Luke 4:18). Among the assurances given to John the Baptist that Jesus was indeed the Messiah was that through Him, "the poor have the gospel preached to them" (Luke 7:22).

It is interesting that many pastors are eager to get "shakers and movers" into their churches. Yet it has been my experience that the financially wealthy are often not the largest givers proportionately. Further, Church history reveals a clear pattern that renewal almost never begins among the wealthy and almost always begins among the working classes and the poor. This is probably a continuation of Jesus' anointing to preach deliverance to the poor.

We must also face the truth that the rich tend to be preoccupied with this world's concerns. This is, no doubt, the reason that Jesus said it is difficult for a rich man to enter the Kingdom of heaven. The Lord was not saying that it was impossible; He was saying that it is a formidable task to wrench the rich from their worldly preoccupations to consider the wooings of another world. Alexander Pope noticed this tendency in his epic *Essay on Man*:

> *The rich is happy in the plenty giv'n,*
> *The poor contents him with the care of Heav'n.*[4]

But the thesis of this book is that, while indeed you can't take it with you, you *can* send it on ahead. The cash and tender of this world can be invested for dividends and returns in the next. When we give for the advance of the gospel, we are investing in the next world. When we give sacrificially to our churches and legitimate ministries, we are laying up treasures in heaven. And, when we sow a godly, serving life, we are sure to reap fantastic returns on our investment, as the next chapter will show.

It has been my privilege to preach in many countries of the world. I've seen firsthand the plight of the world's poor and dispossessed. Everything I know about God and His character convinces me that it is inconceivable that God could be honored by the degrading effects of poverty on the human spirit. It is also clear to any who give history even a slight overview that the gospel has an inherent lift in it. The gospel lifts the crushing loads of guilt, despair, and yes, poverty. Some sociologists have postulated very plausible theories of the tie between the Protestant Reformation and the Industrial Revolution, the first being the cause and the latter being the effect. Others speak of a "Protestant work ethic," stating that life based on glorifying God lifted Europe out of both the economic and spiritual doldrums of the Middle Ages. Undoubtedly these factors were present. God delights in propelling people to their full potential. And no one can reach his full potential without in some way touching his ability to generate income.

I do not wish to over-generalize. And I know that this theory may break down in many ways. But the theory of "seasons" for nations and empires seems to have credibility. Some now theorize that America is declining and is in an inevitable "autumn" of her life. If this is true, it is interesting to note that it comes at a time when the United States is rapidly becoming more secularized. In evangelical terms, we could say that the seed of the gospel was generously planted in the spring of the nation. The fruit of the gospel was reaped in the summer of our existence as a nation. And now, the harvest of the economic blessings being reaped and the summer being past, we have entered the autumn of our civilization.

Following this idea, the seed of the gospel has been planted by the nations of the West in many, if not most, of the Third World nations. Though many of those nations refused the Christian gospel, the message had enough reception that it changed their thinking about themselves. The gospel brought dignity and elevation to previously enslaved peoples. Now the harvest of this gospel seed is beginning to be reaped. And with it comes a dramatic shift in the world economic balance of power. In other words, the gospel has literally blessed the nations.

But now these emerging nations must be cautioned against the same tendencies to greed that trapped America and ended her summer of harvest. Instead of continuing to plant, somewhere we became so gluttonous financially that we began to consume our own seed. Thus, inevitably, the harvest receded and autumn set in.

This is not to say that this trend cannot be reversed. The

Christian is not a pessimistic determinist, convinced that things must take their inevitable course. No, the whole point of the gospel is that, through repentance, God's mercy comes into play and there is renewal and restoration, both personal and national.

Yet success does have a way of undoing people and nations. Richard Niebuhr made the incisive comment that no denomination has ever fully survived its own success. It could be argued that the same might well be said of nations and individuals. So what is the assurance that our blessings will remain blessings and not become our own nooses? If there is a safeguard, it lies in giving God's blessings back to Him. We receive them with gratitude, drink from them with joy, but most importantly, pour them out on others with magnanimity.

Walking the Tightrope

God is a God of wealth and abundance. He evidently created some things merely for the purpose of aesthetics and joy. Scripture teaches that the home of the wise and godly individual is filled with treasure and precious commodities. The Bible teaches us to dispense our blessings unilaterally, pouring out our supply of water on the thirsty with a holy disregard as to who the recipients of our generosity will be. Without question, a vein of prosperity and blessing runs through the Bible. But prosperity is *not* the message; it is merely one tributary of the vast, flowing river of the mercy and love of God.

> *There is a clear purpose in prosperity.*
> *True, God blesses us for the simple reason*
> *that He loves us. But, having blessed us,*
> *He then destines us to be a blessing.*

God promised Abram, "I will bless you and make your

name great." For many contemporary Christians, that would be the end of the covenant of promise. They would put that promise on their refrigerators and revel in the coming blessings. But God added something to that promise: "I will bless you and make your name great: *and you shall be a blessing*" (Gen. 12:2). Abram would be blessed by God so he would have the capacity to bless others. And notice the context of the promise. God promised blessings to Abram as He forcibly turned him away from his protected environment to become the world's first cross-cultural missionary. It is in the arena of spiritual risk and radical obedience that the covenant of blessing is effected.

We must walk the tightrope with delicately balanced understanding regarding prosperity. Wealth is ultimately from God. "The earth is the Lord's and all its fullness . . ." (Ps. 24:1). Yet affluence in and of itself is not to be perceived as God's approval on an individual's life. Nor is economic distress to be viewed as sure evidence of His disapproval. We have all seen the ungodly prosper at the expense of the godly. Remember that Jesus said: "But woe to you who are rich, for you have already received your comfort" (Luke 6:24;NIV). But once again, if current conditions are viewed form an eternal perspective, we know there is coming a day when all inequities will be forever destroyed and true justice will be enacted. To view a temporary financial condition as an indicator of divine approval or disapproval is myopic and distorted.

These are simple, basic thoughts. Yet we often seem to overlook them. Let's review them briefly.

1. *Abject poverty is demeaning and dehumanizing.* God's desire for His creation is blessing though union with Him. And flowing from the inestimable benefits of Calvary are the blessings of living in dignity. "He who did not spare His own Son, but delivered Him up for us all, how shall He not with Him also freely give us all things?" (Rom. 8:32). Consequently, poverty cannot be the will of God. Christians

may, however, lower their standard of living voluntarily to improve their standard of life. Thus, voluntary vows of poverty (as with the Franciscans) and acts of sacrifice are in keeping with the servant motif of genuine Christian living. Such acts remind us that the true riches Jesus spoke of are not material.

Involuntary lack, however, has its origin with the one whose purpose it is to steal, kill, and destroy. In contrast, Jesus Christ has come to give abundant life on every level. I was taught in seminary that one could not take 3 John 2 as a personal promise. That verse says, "Beloved, I pray that you may prosper in all things and be in health, just as your soul prospers." It is correct exegetically to understand that this is an apostolic greeting from John to Gaius, but I believe it is incorrect to deduce from this that the intent cannot be broadened. For one thing, simple, trusting believers *have* taken this prayer as a personal promise through the centuries, and have grown in faith because of it. And I am prone to think that God blesses simple faith far more than enlightened exegesis. Further, if John prayed for this as a good thing for one of God's children, should we not also desire prosperity and health for all His children? Also, if we take the exegetical liberty of personalizing other verses, such as prayers by the apostle Paul for different churches, can we not by the same standard personalize this apostolic benediction?

2. *The roots of financial stress are often complex.* I'm reminded of the time the blind man came to Jesus for healing. Immediately His disciples conjectured simplistic theories regarding the reason for the man's infirmity. "Who sinned," they inquired, "that this man was born blind?" Just so today, Jesus' disciples are prone to ask, "Who sinned?" or "Whose faith was lacking?" when they see those in need. Jesus rebuked His disciples for a spiritual condition more blinding than the man's physical disability. Some Christians seem to think financial stress is a sure sign of God's disfavor.

While this may be the case on rare occasions, such thinking usually exposes a great deal more about the ones asking the questions than those in the financial difficulty. It is true that the Scriptures teach that we are to give a tenth of our incomes to God. This is a token acknowledgment that all we have actually belongs to Him. Yet even when one tithes or gives above the tithe, they must remain a faithful steward over the rest of their finances. It is possible to be faithful in giving but be unfaithful in meeting obligations, investing, or practicing frugality.

Also, some factors producing financial stress are beyond the individual's control. Interest rates are determined by banks and governments. Layoffs are determined by corporate officers. A hike in retail prices is the decision of someone other than ourselves. And all of these must be seen as factors producing financial hardship on perfectly upright, God-fearing people. They are not the result of sin or a mere lack of faith.

3. *Christians are warned against greed and trusting in uncertain riches.* Paul encouraged the young pastor, Timothy, to remind his wealthy parishioners to invest in heaven. "Command those who are rich in this present age not to be haughty, nor to trust in uncertain riches but in the living God, who gives us richly all things to enjoy. Let them do good, that they be rich in good works, ready to give, willing to share, storing up for themselves a good foundation for the time to come, that they may lay hold on eternal life" (1 Tim. 6:17-19).

Like food, money is necessary for survival. But a lust for it, also like food, produces a condition that is both unsightly and unhealthy. Jesus said flatly it is impossible to serve both Him and a pervading materialistic spirit. "No one can serve two masters; for either he will hate the one and love the other, or else he will be loyal to the one and despise the other. You cannot serve God and mammon" (Matt. 6:24).

4. *One must possess wealth to release wealth.* Having warned against flirtation with wealth, the Bible not only allows Christians to gain riches, it actually encourages them to do so. Why? Because in any dimension, you cannot impart what you do not possess. It is the impoverished who are trapped and stymied in their ability to bless others. So an entire book of the Bible (the Book of Proverbs) gives a great deal of space to financial principles intended to generate wealth. This wealth is produced for the express purpose of giving a good measure of it away in blessing. Thus the cycle of blessing is perpetuated: Give and it shall be given to you so you may give again in increased proportion.

5. *The believer's life is to be marked by generosity.* In Christ's new order, the most vulnerable are not the risk-takers but the self-protective. "For whoever desires to save his life will lose it, but whoever loses his life for My sake and the gospel's will save it" (Mark 8:35). The exciting irony of the Christian adventure is that under the New Covenant we give to receive, we profit by losing, we find our lives by laying them down. The follower of Jesus is first a producer, not a consumer. His emphasis is serving, not being served. The disciple remembers the words of his Lord, "It is more blessed to give than to receive" (Acts 20:35).

As I work with Third World church leadership one of the first principles I teach is the blessedness of giving. Many times nationals have been conditioned to expect financial help from the "rich American brothers." Thus, they foster a receiving instead of a giving mentality. I am convinced that the first step out of poverty is to break this "give me" syndrome. We recite the words of the Lord Jesus together from Luke 6:38 and Acts 20:35. Then I challenge them to "find a way, every day, to give something to God and something to people." Many national workers have told me stories of personal liberation as they began to explore this biblical way of living. It *is* more blessed to give than to receive.

6. *Good stewardship over present resources is a prerequisite to greater blessings.* This holds true both in the proportion and the kind of blessings. In the parable of the talents, Jesus sets forth the principle of faithfulness as the qualification for greater usefulness and greater blessings. In the story, the master commended his steward for faithful and wise investment of his current resources. Then came the reward. " 'Well done, my good servant!' his master replied. 'Because you have been trustworthy in a very small matter, take charge of ten cities' " (Luke 19:17;NIV).

This principle also holds true for greater kinds of blessing. We must be faithful stewards of, as Jesus termed it, unrighteous mammon so we will know the true value of things material and *supra*material. "If you have not been faithful in the unrighteous mammon, who will commit to your trust the true riches?" the Lord asks (Luke 16:11). The way we handle money is an indicator of the way we will handle that which is truly valuable.

There is a purpose in prosperity. Our attitude toward and stewardship of finances either qualifies or disqualifies us for eternal treasures.

In today's squeamish economy, people are searching for a safe place to invest that will still yield impressive returns.

There is still such a place.

5

Heaven: The Most Solid Investment on Earth

These all died in faith, not having received the promises, but having seen them afar off were assured of them, embraced them and confessed that they were strangers and pilgrims on the earth (Heb. 11:13).

October 19, 1987. Some call it the day the Yuppie culture died. On that panic-riddled day the stock market plummeted more than 500 points.

For many, fortunes were lost. For others, businesses were lost. For still others, hopes were lost. And for some materialists, minds were lost as their religion of greed failed them.

Fear stuck in the stomachs of thousands with the realization that lifetimes of careful investing were being mercilessly abolished hour by agonizing hour. How could this have happened? After all, had we not been assured that such a scenario was impossible? Weren't we taught in Economics 101 that the market now had built-in checks and balances that would buttress it infallibly against a repeat of Doomsday 1929? After all, this was *America*. This was the *Reagan* era.

It would be misleading to suggest that only the ungodly temporarily lost their economic equilibrium. Individual believers suffered terribly. Families' prospects were hurt. Christian ministries reeled from the double barrel blast of Christians' diminished financial capabilities and widely publicized scandals. From a natural viewpoint, dread was in order.

As we have seen, the Bible cautions against the tendency to wrap our hearts around money and things it can buy. "Do not love the world or the things in the world. If anyone loves the world, the love of the Father is not in him" (1 John 2:15). Jesus taught by word and humble example, "One's life does not consist in the abundance of the things he possesses" (Luke 12:15). The Lord told the story of a man who was so affluent he didn't know where to put his money. He finally determined to tear down his barns and build bigger ones (no doubt with higher fences to better isolate him from the plight of the poor). Jesus blatantly calls him a shortsighted fool and warns, "So is he who lays up treasures for himself, and is not rich toward God" (Luke 12:21).

The Prosperity Message and Economic Uncertainty

If these reminders seem brusque, perhaps it is because I am writing this chapter from a small wooden desk in rural India. When the electricity works I use my host's typewriter (on which was slapped a large tax since it is a "luxury item"). When the current is cut without notice (a frequent occurrence), I write longhand. As I look outside I see grass huts, low caste workers who farm the fields for less than $200 per year, and an ox-driven cart carrying the day's harvest to market.

"But," you may protest, "that's not the real world." Then why is ours the "real world"? Only a fraction of this planet's population knows our world, complete with its savings accounts and pension plans. Two billion people live in theirs with its constricting and unflinching needs.

My heart reaches out to the people I see outside my window. I look at their grass and bamboo dwellings and wonder what happens when typhoon season comes. I ponder what it's like to drink only typhoid-infested water. How does food taste that is prepared on an open fire fueled by dried cow dung? What is it like to have children with intellectual promise who cannot possibly hope for a decent education? How deeply dehumanizing is it to wake day after day, year after year, to these same conditions as your parents did before you and as your children will after you? And in the midst of such intense, immediate despair, what is it like to have no hope of heaven, no good news of salvation, no forgiveness, no Jesus?

> *When things are viewed from both a global and an eternal perspective, many of our preconceived notions must bow to reality.*

Most of the world now, including the United States, is in economic disarray. Jesus predicted such a time when there would be "distress of nations, with perplexity" (Luke 21:25). The inference from the original language is that there is no way out. It is no longer the religious fanatics and self-styled prophets who lead the parade announcing doom. Ph.D.'s in economics and sociology postulate that we may have reached the point of no return. With a three to four trillion dollar national debt, it would seem that we are literally drowning in red ink.

Our national sins (as well as our personal ones) certainly justify the judgment of God. As Christians, however, we must not give in to despair. God has a propensity for mercy when His children cry to Him in repentance. Throughout history, God has relented from even His pronounced judgment in response to the sincere cries of the penitent. I am frankly encouraged when I see the tens of thousands who are being gathered in concerts of prayer across America. This can only signal coming blessing, in spite of the storm clouds.

It is true that many godly people are prophesying doom. Even if they are hearing correctly, it is not unprecedented for God to take a merciful course in response to brokenness and prayer. God has promised, "The instant I speak concerning a nation and concerning a kingdom, to pluck up, to pull down, and to destroy it, if that nation against whom I have spoken turns from its evil, I will relent of the disaster that I thought to bring upon it" (Jer. 18:7-8).

Through all our heartbreaking crises God is speaking clearly. He is calling His church to repentance and holiness. He is wooing us away from the lust of the flesh, the lust of the eyes, and the pride of life. That is why a new look at an eternal perspective is, I believe, so very timely. God is calling us to a new definition of success.

William James, a noted psychologist at the turn of the century, possessed keen insight into the coming crisis of moral weakness that would confront America. In a letter to H.G. Wells dated September 11, 1906, he spoke almost prophetically of our battle of will. Though he used words we may deem unacceptable, he pointedly blasted "the moral flabbiness born of the exclusive worship of the bitch-goddess *success*. That — with the squalid cash interpretation put on the word success — is our national disease."

No preacher could have been more on target. Now God himself is calling His church back to a standard of righteousness. A ground swell of cries for justice and righteousness can now be heard throughout the land. To preserve any semblance of civilization as we have known it, there must be a moral revolution.

Jesus Christ is always in the business of reconciliation and restoration. Just as the powerful Wesleyan movement swept Britain in a tide of salvation and sanctification, the times cry out for another, even larger dose of biblical holiness. I'm convinced it can come — and quickly. What has taken the devil years to unravel slowly, Jesus Christ can restore in minutes. The road to true contrition may be long, but repentance itself happens in a moment. Then God's mercy responds immediately and restoration begins.

A little boy was telling his classmates about the wonderful difference in his family since his father had become a Christian. Before his conversion, his father had terrorized the family with his alcoholism — even breaking lamps and chairs in his tirades. But now he had been delivered by Christ and peace prevailed in the home. He even used the money once spent on beer to refurnish their home.

The boy's teacher, a secular humanist, overheard his happy testimony. Wishing to "enlighten" him, she said, "Johnny, you can't hope for a real change. Your father has just had a traumatic religious experience. Besides, you can't believe in a religion based on the Bible with all its myths. You can't possibly believe the story about Jesus turning the water into wine," the teacher admonished him.

"Why shouldn't I?" Johnny replied. "When Jesus came to my house He turned beer into furniture!"

Jesus Christ is the radical reformer — of people, of families, of nations, of destinies. He wants to invade your life and your thinking, even as you read. He stands ready to adjust our perspective — to His.

Investing in Eternity

Henry Ward Beecher, a famous minister of the last century, said, "Success is full of promise till men get it; and then it is a last year's nest, from which the bird has flown." This elusive quality of the fulfillment of hopes is a typical phenomenon here on earth.

But not so with heaven's rewards. They are permanent and teeming with undiminished joy. Eighty times the Bible speaks of rewards. Here is just a sampling of the proddings of Scripture to seek heaven's non-depreciating accolades.

"Surely there is a reward for the righteous, surely He is God who judges in the earth" (Ps. 58:11).

"The wicked man does deceptive work, but to him who sows righteousness will be a sure reward" (Prov. 11:18).

"Behold, the Lord God shall come with a strong hand, and His arm shall rule for Him; behold, His reward is with Him" (Isa. 40:10).

"Blessed are you when they revile and persecute you, and say all kinds of evil against you falsely for My sake. Rejoice and be exceedingly glad, for great is your reward in heaven" (Matt. 5:11-12).

"But when you do a charitable deed, do not let your left hand know what your right hand is doing, that your charitable deed may be in secret; and your Father who sees in secret will Himself reward you openly" (Matt. 6:3-4).

"But you, when you pray, go into your room, and when you have shut your door, pray to your Father who is in the secret place, and your Father who sees in secret will reward you openly" (Matt. 6:6).

"For the Son of Man will come in the glory of His Father with His angels, and then He will reward each according to his works" (Matt. 16:27).

"For whoever gives you a cup of water to drink in My name, because you belong to Christ, assuredly, I say to you, he will by no means lose his reward" (Mark 9:41).

"But love your enemies, do good, and lend, hoping for nothing in return; and your reward will be great" (Luke 6:35).

"And whatever you do, do it heartily, as to the Lord and not to men, knowing that from the Lord you will receive the reward of the inheritance; for you serve the Lord Christ" (Col. 3:23-24).

"But recall the former days in which, after you were illuminated, you endured a great struggle with sufferings: partly while you were made a spectacle both by reproaches and tribulations, and partly while you became companions of those who were so treated; for you had compassion on me in my chains, and joyfully accepted the plundering of your goods, knowing that you have a better and an enduring possession for yourselves in heaven. Therefore do not cast away your confidence, which has great reward" (Heb. 10:32-35).

"Look to yourselves, that we do not lose those things we worked for, but that we may receive a full reward" (2 John 1:8).

"And, behold, I am coming quickly, and My reward is with Me, to give to every one according to his work" (Rev. 22:12).

These injunctions boil down to seeing beyond the present to the eternal, loving God supremely and serving people as an expression of our love for God. There is a payoff worth waiting for.

The Prize of the High Calling

In Oswald Chambers' words, "We are to give our utmost for His highest." As we yield to the prompting of the Holy Spirit, we are laying up spiritual treasure. The only time we have in which to invest is now, this present moment. We can do nothing about the past except give it to Jesus. Tomorrow is not promised to us. Now is our opportunity. We must realize that our opportunities are fleeting. In view of the brevity of time we should pray, as David did, "So teach us to number our days, that we may gain a heart of wisdom" (Ps. 90:12). And what will be the result of a heart of wisdom? A prudent walk before the Lord and a conscientious investing of time. "See then that you walk circumspectly, not as fools but as wise, redeeming the time, because the days are evil" (Eph. 5:15-16).

And as we invest our days for Him, through worship of Him and service to people, God's law of sowing and reaping goes into effect. God has so ordained that whatever we sow, we reap. Sometimes very soon, sometimes years later, sometimes in eternity. But the principle always holds true. We reap what we sow.

A little-known story of two evangelical leaders well illustrates this immutable principle. One night in the mid-1940s, a young college graduate was thumbing a ride to Los Angeles. Not a Christian, his goal in life was to become a millionaire and live in the Bel Air district of Beverly Hills. But this night, the Oklahoma collegian was short on cash.

A man picked up the hitchhiker and they began to talk. "Do you know anywhere in Los Angeles I can spend the night?" the traveler inquired.

"I think so," replied the driver. "There's a guy named Dawson Trotman who's putting up some sailors at his house, teaching them the Bible or something. Maybe he'd find you a bed tonight."

And so it was that, on his first night in California, Bill Bright became the recipient of Dawson Trotman's hospitality. Little did either of them realize that within a few years they would both head massively influential Christian ministries.

A decade after that California night, Trotman's Navigators were in a race against time to purchase Glen Eyrie, their proposed Colorado Springs headquarters. Bill Bright, by now head of the fledgling Campus Crusade for Christ ministry, personally gave sacrificially and wrote 5,000 friends of his new organization asking them to help. The Navigators were able to make the purchase.

Dawson's kindness, sown a decade earlier, was reaped in kindness sown by Bill Bright and Campus Crusade to the sister ministry of the Navigators. This beautiful picture of deference and secure leadership on both of their parts is a potent reminder to us today. Little did Dawson and Lila Trotman realize that one night's room and board, given in Jesus' name, would yield help in the form of financial assistance when they needed it. Just so, many cups of cold water, given in the natural course of things with no thought of reward, will be returned in invaluable treasure — both in this life and the next.[1]

Whenever anyone of prominence says, in effect, "This above all else," it is wise to pay close attention to what the "one thing" is. For instance, in Shakespeare's *Hamlet*, he advises, "This above all: to thine own self be true." More ancient is the counsel attributed to the Seven Sages inscribed at the Delphic Oracle some 600 years before Christ: "Know thyself."

Sound advice from time-honored wisdom: *Know* yourself. *Be true* to yourself. But there comes from the pen of a Jewish scholar-turned-Apostle an even greater piece of wisdom: Forget the past and *give* yourself to attaining the heavenly prize ahead at the end of life's race.

"Brethren, I do not count myself to have apprehended; but one thing I do, forgetting those things which are behind and reaching forward to those things which are ahead, I press toward the goal for the prize of the upward call of God in Christ Jesus" (Phil. 3:13-14). This is ultimate success.

So press on, with all your strength. When the winner stretches forward and finally breaks the tape, it'll be worth every effort.

But what about the very personal pain of the present?

6

If Healing Is Delayed

*For our light affliction, which is but for a
moment, is working for us a far more exceeding and eternal weight of glory, while we do
not look at the things which are seen, but at
the things which are not seen. For the things
which are seen are temporary, but the things
which are not seen are eternal* (2 Cor. 4:17-
18).

I am the product of a miracle. When I was born neither
my mother nor I was expected to live. At birth I weighed
under four pounds. As my mother was in labor, my father
waited anxiously with a family friend, an evangelist who
was powerfully used in overseas healing and miracle cru-
sades. His name is T.L. Osborn. Just as I was being born,
Reverend Osborn was strongly impressed to pray for my life
and my mother's. Turning to my father, he said, "Warren,
we've got to rebuke the spirit of death right now."

God intervened. What appeared to be certain death for
both mother and child was turned into victory and honor for
the Lord. Today, over four decades later, I enjoy consis-

tently good health. And my mother, in her seventies, retains good health, as well.

The knowledge that God spared my life at birth has been a strong undercurrent of "knowing" deep inside my spirit. I never question that He has a specific will for my life, and death cannot take me until His work for me is accomplished. Jim Elliot, martyred by Auca tribesmen in 1956, put it this way: "I am immortal until my work is finished." Every believer who knows his times are in God's hand has the same assurance.

I share that story to go on record as a witness and participant in the present-day healing power of God. I have experienced the healing virtue of Christ numerous times in my own body. And I've witnessed the dramatic effects of Christ's healing touch in answer to believing prayer. At the core of who I am I know that healing and miracles are to accompany the preaching of the gospel. Jesus heals people to verify the fact that He is the living Son of God. But He also heals people just because He loves them.

Having said this, however, I wish to help those whose healing has been delayed — though I sometimes wonder if the people who do not receive healing in this life are among those who wait most longingly for heaven and the new life to be given them there. By admitting that some healings will be received only in heaven I will no doubt receive criticism from those who say I lack faith and am insulting the promises of God. If in any way this is in my heart, I ask forgiveness, not from my critics, but from God himself. The desire of my life is to stimulate faith, not diminish it. But, because of the ministry in my trust, I have been uniquely privileged to view the issue of healing from a dual perspective. As an evangelist, I have seen remarkable healings and miracles in answer to prayer. But I have also seen those who have left in the same wheelchairs they came in. Toward them I must minister pastorally. Has God failed? Has their faith failed? What can you do if healing is delayed? And where does heaven fit into this discussion?

Is God at Fault?

Let's get one thing straight from the outset: God is good. He does not inflict sickness on anyone. And since God never inflicts sickness on anyone, it cannot be said that sickness itself glorifies God. Now the godly character that is often produced as a result of suffering does glorify God. The very physical weakness we disdain often casts us at the mercy of God's power. When the body is weak there is less chance for an unholy brew of flesh and spirit in ministry. The inner person of the spirit must compensate for the weakness of the flesh. So while sickness itself is never God-honoring, the effects of sickness on the teachable Christian often are. This is not to say that God allows us to be sick to "teach us a lesson." Remember, His nature is kind and good.

> *God is the master strategist who delights in watching the devil overplay his hand in his tactics against us. What the devil meant for evil, God reverses for our good.*

When faith is exercised, the result many times is a lifting of the oppressing circumstances or a healing from tormenting disease. But God may choose to honor our faith, not by releasing us from our difficulties, but by developing Christlikeness in us through our difficulties. After all, how can we become like Jesus unless we too know something about sorrow and become acquainted with grief?

Some of the most forceful teachings on faith in the Bible come from the pen of the apostle Paul. And his experience backed up his teaching. This mighty Apostle who cast out demons and whose hands were a transmitter for healings from Christ was no less a person of faith because God sovereignly chose not to remove his thorn in the flesh. Paul turned this tormenting deficit into one of his greatest assets.

"Concerning this thing," Paul said, "I pleaded with the Lord three times that it might depart from me. And He said to me, 'My grace is sufficient for you, for My strength is made perfect in weakness.' Therefore most gladly I will rather boast in my infirmities, that the power of Christ may rest upon me. Therefore I take pleasure in infirmities, in reproaches, in needs, in persecutions, in distresses, for Christ's sake. For when I am weak, then I am strong" (2 Cor. 12:8-10).

And we dare not miss one additional benefit from present sufferings. They make us more desirous of heaven. This is not escapism. Provided we keep sight of today's responsibilities here to God and others, to long for heaven is both healthy and scriptural. It is no more unnatural than a soldier stationed in a war zone who longs to be home. He stays at his post because he was stationed there by a higher power. But his heart is back in the States. Just so, the Christian is often placed on assignment in less than desirable conditions by his commander in chief. But his heart is in another place, his true home where pain, suffering, and war are non-existent.

Is My Faith Weak?

So we understand that if a believer who has asked for healing remains infirmed, God is not the culprit. But the question that haunts most Christians who are ill isn't whether or not God has failed. They love and know Him well enough to know that it is impossible for Him to fail. The question that plagues the Christian with an illness is whether or not he or she has failed.

"Perhaps there is sin in my life and that's why I'm not healed," they reason. Yet, if we follow this train of thought, no one could be either healed or saved. It is precisely because we *have* sinned that we need a Saviour. Clearly it is God's unmerited grace that brings salvation. It follows that every transaction between God and people is based on God's grace, not the individual's performance. He saves —

and heals — not because we are good, but because He is good.

"But," the beleaguered believer continues to probe, "perhaps my level of faith was not high enough to be healed." But then we place "faith in God" in two categories: saving faith and healing faith. We believe we have sufficient faith to trust Christ for salvation but somehow lack sufficient faith to trust Him for healing. This is an unscriptural dichotomy. To be saved one must place his total faith in the power of Jesus Christ to save him. And to be healed one must do the same thing. Here many believers battle confusion, for they see no difference between the level of faith they exercised for their salvation and the level of faith they are exercising for their healing. Yet, while their sins are forgiven and gone, their sickness remains. There must be something more involved than a lack of faith.

First Things First

There are many roots of sickness and disease, and I believe that a lack of faith for healing can be one reason for continuing illness — but only one. Clearly other dynamics are often involved.

Most predominant are physical roots to sickness that have nothing to do with one's faith or lack of it. To illustrate, many physical illnesses may be traced to the root causes of obesity and worry. These two debilitators are not cured by the prayer of faith. They are cured by repentance and commensurate acts of obedience.

A woman may stand in a healing line expecting deliverance from high blood pressure. If, however, the high blood pressure is caused by hypertension which in turn is caused by worry, the first step for the woman is not faith for healing but repentance from the sin of worry. Then faith does come into play. She must henceforth learn to trust Jesus Christ fully for all of life's stresses. Then her faith will make her whole.

A man may request prayer for the healing of heart

disease. But if he is 60 pounds overweight, the antidote once again is not faith but repentance. Having brought his eating habits under the lordship of Christ, he can then have unhindered faith for healing because his conscience will no longer condemn him.

Then there are the tougher questions with far more elusive answers. Why was David Watson, an anointed leader in the British renewal, stricken with cancer? Why was he allowed to linger and suffer before eventually succumbing to death? Why was Jack Coe, powerful healing evangelist of the fifties, taken at the height of his ministry? Why were unbelievers allowed to mock the "healer" who died? (How reminiscent of the scoffers at the cross: "He healed others — himself He cannot heal.") Why did Howard Conatser, unrivaled leader of Southern Baptist Charismatics, die of cancer only a few years after he was, according to his own reports, raised from the dead after an out-of-the-body experience with the Lord in heaven? Why did my own father, the most godly man I ever met, die a seemingly premature, painful death at age 44?

The Rest of the Story

One could take an entire book to postulate "answers" to such questions. And, at best, our hypotheses would be conjectural and incomplete. This much we know: Our world is imperfect, tainted with sin and its effects. The Kingdom has come into our hearts but it is not yet fully manifested on earth. Yes, we have seen great and mighty things. We have witnessed miracles. I have seen the crippled walk, the deaf rejoice in restored hearing, the blind see. Yet some unanswered questions will remain until we see Jesus. To those unanswered questions we must acknowledge an element of mystery: we know in part. Yet it is precisely this element of mystery that makes God transcendent. His ways are beyond us. " 'For My thoughts are not your thoughts, nor are your ways My ways,' says the Lord. 'For as the heavens are higher than the earth, so are My ways higher than your ways, and My thoughts than your thoughts' " (Isa. 55:8-9). "Who has directed the Spirit of the Lord, or as His counselor has taught Him?" (Isa. 40:13).

To put it frankly, there are some of His ways that our hearts may question but that He is not obligated to answer. At least not now. He is God. Period. For this reason, some of His actions regarding us can only be termed mysterious. Yet all are birthed in infinite love.

It is almost a matter of pride among Spirit-filled Christians that we don't "put God in a box." We deride the liberal influences of rationalism. Yet some "faith" teaching clearly does "put God in a box": "Do this and you'll get that," "Make this confession and you'll receive what you want." These are simplistic formulas of a system built on rationalism. The ways of Almighty God are more complex, more mysterious than that. We insult His holy, omnipotent character when we reduce His options to our wishes. If we put the right number of quarters into the Coke machine we expect to receive a Coke. But the analogy cannot be carried over that if we make the right confession or believe on the right level we will automatically get what we want. For unlike the soda machine, God is neither mindless nor mechanical. He is omniscient and personal. And while God is never irrational, He is not rationalistic. Sometimes His ways transcend our ability to reason.

We must also take into account the fact that our bodies are not yet redeemed. God's redemptive process begins in the spirit and works progressively outward. At conversion we are saved from the penalty of sin — that is, eternal separation from God. As we yield to the Holy Spirit we are saved from the power of sin as the soul (comprised of mind, emotions, and will) comes under the lordship of Christ. Ultimately, we will be saved from the very presence of sin. Then the deadly effects of sin will be reversed and our bodies will be raised incorruptible (1 Cor. 15:52).

Every now and then the mini-heresy that we have

already received our glorified bodies crops up. It is based on the assertion of Jesus in John 11:26 that those who believe in Him will never die. All who truly believe, so the teaching goes, enter into a non-ending life free from sickness and death.

When I was growing up, a pastor's wife in our town fell prey to this doctrine. Her husband challenged her. "So you already have your glorified body?" he asked.

"I'm convinced of it," she retorted. He looked straight into her magnified eyes.

"Then why are you wearing those glasses?"

The Bible clearly teaches that we are still "eagerly waiting for the adoption, the redemption of our body" (Rom. 8:23). The body remains under the curse of sin though the spirit has been delivered through the new birth. "Even though our outward man is perishing, yet the inward man is being renewed day by day" (2 Cor. 4:16).

While the believer may wrestle to understand a healing that is delayed, healing for the believer in Jesus is never denied. "By His stripes we are healed" (Isa. 53:5). Many afflicted are healed immediately. Others are healed over a period of time. All Christians are forever healed in the resurrection of their bodies. If we maintain an eternal perspective, we can look forward to that.

Even the believer who faces terminal illness need never fear. Jesus himself knows what it feels like to die. And He declared: "Because I live, you will live also" (John 14:19).

Until death, the believer trusts the stripes of Jesus for healing. But, if death comes, then through and past death the believer continues to trust the blood of Christ. Healing will come.

7

O Death, Where Is Your Sting?

For if we live, we live to the Lord; and if we die, we die to the Lord. Therefore, whether we live or die, we are the Lord's (Rom. 14:8).

After her examination, the family doctor asked Mrs. Thompson to be seated in his office. Dr. Judson chose his words carefully. "I want to be up front with you, Mrs. Thompson." He paused and drew an extended breath. "We've discovered cancer in advanced stages throughout your body. We will treat it as best we can. But, barring a miracle, your days are numbered."

Mrs. Thompson's life seemed to flash before her. In a few seconds time she sped through the emotional roller-coaster of shock, disbelief, anger, and fear. Then a familiar peace steadied her maddening ride.

"Dr. Judson," she began, "you say my days are numbered." Wiping her tears and looking up with a smile, she announced, "Well, Doctor, so are yours."

The Bible teaches emphatically that each of us has an allotted time on earth — time enough (however brief it may seem) to recognize our need for our Saviour, Jesus Christ. Sadly, not everyone comes to this conclusion, thinking instead that he or she has found another "comparable" answer.

The fact that we live in an age baptized in relativism was brought home to me forcibly not long ago as I was sharing my faith in Christ with a man next to me on a plane. After listening patiently to my presentation of the gospel, he replied, "That may be the truth for you, but not for me. I have another truth."

Another truth! A generation of "situation ethics" has led many Americans to believe that truth itself is relative. This was also graphically portrayed by the young man who commented to me, "I don't have to worry about hell. I don't believe in it."

My reply to him was that no amount of belief or disbelief in hell would make it disappear. The fact remains.

In the same way, many people form theories about death based on their wishes instead of facts. Yet the Bible gives clear facts concerning death. Since death is sure for everyone (barring the return of Christ for His church), wisdom cries that we prepare for this inevitable event.

Three Facts about Death

A single verse of Scripture gives a concise overview of the Bible's teaching on death. Hebrews 9:27 says, "It is appointed for men to die once, but after this the judgment."

From this passage three important facts emerge concerning death. First, death happens once. "It is appointed for men to die *once* . . . ." The only time in which to invest for eternity is now, in this life. The current fad of belief in reincarnation is but one more tragic deception. Whether one buys into this aberration of reality by way of the "New Age movement" or an ancient religious system, the fact remains that people die once, not many times. Reservations for heaven must be made in this life, for this is the only one there is. How ironic that an old beer commercial contains more theological truth than some contemporary religious fads. "You only go around once in life!"

Second, death is not a termination; neither is it entrance into "soul sleep," as some profess. Rather, it is a momentary interruption in an ongoing life. Death merely transfers us out of one sphere of existence to another. But life itself goes on. "It is appointed for men to die once, but *after this . . . .*"

I remember several years ago when Soviet Chief Leonid Brezhnev died. I remember the tragic scene from *Time* magazine as his wife bent over the coffin, giving her husband one last kiss. As leader of his country's Communist party, Mr. Brezhnev led the largest atheistic political system in the world. As I viewed the picture I wondered what it would be like to face death with absolutely no hope of heaven.

Third, death is followed by judgment. "It is appointed for men to die once, but after this *the judgment.*" The theory of universal salvation is rejected by the Scriptures. The unrepentant will face judgment and eternity without Christ.

The friend of a deceased atheist came to the funeral home to pay his respects. As he looked at the corpse of his friend, he shook his head and said, "Poor Bob. He's all dressed up with no place to go."

But the Scripture teaches that the unrepentant do indeed have somewhere to go: a place of torment where "their worm does not die and the fire is not quenched" (Mark 9:48). This alternative to heaven is the eternal dwelling of those who reject the forgiveness offered in Jesus Christ. John Milton described it in his epic, *Paradise Lost*:

> *A dungeon horrible on all sides round,*
> *As one great furnace, flamed; yet from those flames*
> *No light, but rather darkness visible*
> *Serv'd only to discover sights of woe*

Regions of sorrow, doleful shades, where peace
And rest can never dwell, hope never comes
That comes to all; but torture without end.[1]

The Christian and Death

As a minister, I probably attend more funerals than most people. And I can tell you this — there is as much difference between the attitudes of Christians and unbelievers toward death as there is between light and darkness, heaven and hell.

For the non-Christian, death is a destroyer. But for the Christian, death is a door. For the non-Christian, death is a deceiver. But for the Christian, death is a deliverance. Freed from the body's earthbound limitations, the transported Christian enters a realm where there are no limits. Christians, when confronted with death, smile through their tears. Why? Because they know that the angel of death does not get the last word; death — though a vicious enemy — does not win the battle. Christians face the raw, coarse realities of death, feeling all its chilling effects, and, like the movie figure Rocky after being pelted with the worst his opponent could deliver, say to death, "You're not so tough. You're not so bad."

Scripture says that "the path of the just is like the shining sun, that shines ever brighter unto the perfect day" (Prov. 4:18). The Christian knows that death ushers him immediately into the secure presence of Jesus. And the believer longs for and anticipates this homegoing.

How wonderfully different from the general prescription society gives for dealing with death. It drugs the dying until death, then drugs the living to make it through the funeral. It seems significant that Jesus refused to take the pain-killing drink offered Him while He was dying. Instead of numbing reality, He chose to taste the undiluted bile of death for himself and for every person (Heb. 2:9). Of course, I am *not* saying that Christians should deny themselves medications when needed. I am saying that we are able, by faith in Jesus Christ, to take the worst death can dish out and still come away victorious.

David Watson said, "The Church is the only society on earth that never loses a member through death! As a Christian I believe not just in life *after* death, but in life *through* death."[2] For the follower of Jesus, the future is always better and brighter, even if death is part of the future. Such an assurance should make the believer both a realist and an optimist, no matter what the current crisis.

Some Christians today seem to think that dying would be evidence of some spiritual lack. They talk of praying for the Lord to return before they die. Of course all of us should have hearts filled with expectancy concerning Christ's return. But do such statements sometimes belie a fear of death? Charles Spurgeon, great preacher of the last century, said he actually looked forward to dying. "What could be more sacred than the experience of dying in Jesus?" he asked. Spurgeon believed the death of a Christian to be the ultimate Christian experience. Just imagine what it will be like to be personally escorted from this world to the next by Jesus Christ!

In fact, the Christian never tastes the full dregs of death. Jesus Christ has done that for us. Jesus said that the one who believes in Him will never die. And it's true, though our physical bodies will one day cease to function, we will escape death's full effects. Having left the earthly sphere, we will be instantly in the presence of the Lord. Life is interrupted but not terminated.

An aged Christian lay on her deathbed, just a few hours away from eternity. Her pastor came to comfort and encourage her. "Young man," she said with a confident smile, "I have no fear coming to this river of death. My Father owns the land on both sides of the river. I'm just transferring to His land on the other side."

This longing for a permanent home, far from producing morbid pessimists, has an extremely healthy effect on our lives here and now. This is not a death wish. Rather, it is a "life wish," a desire to be with the Lord. Vance Havner, a renowned preacher, is now home with the Lord. He not only lived but preached until he was almost 90. He often mentioned, comically yet truthfully, "The hope of death is what's kept me alive so long!"

I believe the death of the righteous has an illustrative counterpart in nature. In my first pastorate, while I was in college in Arkansas, I would drive through the Ozarks in the fall of the year, reveling in the beauty of God's creation and communing with Him. I knew the trees would be cold and dead in a few weeks. But at that point, just before death, they were ablaze with spectacular color.

This visual aid reminds us that the greatest brilliance, spiritually and otherwise, in a believer's life is often just prior to death. This display of color and life is a final testimony on this earth that our mighty God is also faithful. This covenant-keeping God has promised that His faithfulness extends as long as there is seedtime and harvest, winter and summer, as long as there are seasons (Gen. 8:22). No wonder the Bible says, "Precious in the sight of the Lord is the death of His saints" (Ps. 116:15). Even in the process of dying, a unique beauty unfolds. And through it the Christian gives striking testimony to the faithfulness of his God.

When Loved Ones Die

The confidence that we are redemptively connected to the never-ending life of Christ has the power to steady the Christian through any difficulty. Because of this assurance in Jesus, not only can we face the prospects of our own deaths, we can get up off the bed of grief and live again after the death of a loved one.

When I was 15 my father died. Along with my mother and sisters I went through months of heartbreak and agonizing grief. But I was never without the assurance of God's presence. And one day, several months after my father's death, I awoke with the acute awareness of birds singing outside my window. While the sorrow was still there, cold refreshing rushes of hope ran over my soul. I knew, in spite of the terrible loss, we had a future.

> *For the trusting believer, no matter how dark the night, morning always follows mourning.*

"Weeping may endure for a night, but joy comes in the morning" (Ps. 30:5). For the unbeliever, life itself is in the process of unwinding. But not so for the Christian. After the Cross, the Resurrection. After night, day. After death, life. After despair, hope. Man's time cycles start with light and end with night. Not so with God. "The evening and the morning were the first day." Notice the sequence. Always with Him the best is yet to be.

It is impossible to describe fully the inner peace of Jesus' comfort during grief. Perhaps it can only be illustrated. One well-known story that beautifully illustrates this divine aid is the story of Horatio G. Spafford. Mr. Spafford was a successful Chicago lawyer who enjoyed a close friendship with D.L. Moody, Ira Sankey, and several other Evangelical leaders of his day. In 1873, upon the advice of the family physician, for the benefit of his wife's health, he planned a European trip for his family. At the last minute, he was unable to accompany his wife and four daughters due to business developments. So while Mr. Spafford stayed in Chicago, he sent his family, as scheduled, on the SS *Ville du Havre* in November 1873. He anticipated joining them in a few days.

On November 22, the *Ville du Havre* was struck by the *Lochearn*, an English ship, and sank 12 minutes later. Mrs. Spafford was saved. All four daughters perished. On December 1, the survivors landed at Cardiff, Wales. Mrs. Spafford cabled her husband, "Saved alone."

Soon Spafford left by ship to meet his wife. On the high

seas, near the scene of the tragedy, he wrote this hymn:

When peace, like a river, attendeth my way,
When sorrows like sea billows roll;
Whatever my lot, Thou hast taught me to say,
"It is well, it is well with my soul."

Though Satan should buffet, though trials should come,
Let this blest assurance control,
That Christ has regarded my helpless estate,
And hath shed His own blood for my soul.

And, Lord, haste the day when the faith shall be sight,
The clouds be rolled back as a scroll,
The trump shall resound and the Lord shall descend,
"Even so," it is well with my soul.[3]

This prospect of a glad reunion at the feet of Jesus has buttressed the hopes of millions through the centuries. Death is never the final word.

Lasting Influence

The apostle Paul was able to come to the end of his life and announce to his longtime friend Timothy, "For I am already being poured out as a drink offering, and the time of my departure is at hand. I have fought the good fight, I have finished the race, I have kept the faith" (2 Tim. 4:6-7). In essence, Paul was saying, "I have accomplished God's will for my life." Facing death, nothing is more reassuring than that. George W. Truett, longtime pastor said, "Success in life is simply to know the will of God and to do it." Paul was beaten, spat on, shipwrecked. Some think his wife deserted him. He was the victim of verbal abuse. Fellow Christians impugned his motives. But his life was a success. He knew God's will for him — and did it.

Some time ago I stood in the small room in John Wesley's house in London where he died. Having lived almost 90 years he turned the tide of a decadent nation and was the catalyst for spiritual renewal. Even some secular historians attribute him with saving England from the kind of blood bath that was drenching France. Wesley's last words, shortly before he drifted into eternity, were, "The best of all is, God is with us!"

David Brainerd's short life of piety left a lasting impression on the Church. His life of prayer and missionary passion remains a model and challenge. Dying at Northampton on October 9, 1747, his final words were: "I am almost in eternity; I long to be there. My work is done. I have done with my friends — all the world is nothing to me. Oh, to be in heaven to praise and glorify God with His holy angels!"

When we think of Charles Dickens we immediately think of his legacy of great books like *Oliver Twist, David Copperfield,* and *A Christmas Carol.* But his most lasting legacy is the inheritance recorded in his will. He said, "I commit my soul to the mercy of God, through our Lord and Saviour Jesus Christ, and I exhort my dear children humbly to try and guide themselves by the teaching of the New Testament."[4]

My own father retained confidence in Jesus to the end of his life. His influence stretched to many nations as he led the church he pastored in giving 50 percent of its income to world missions. As he was dying he looked at the attending nurse in the hospital and smiled. "Good-bye," he said. "Thank You, Jesus." With that, he was transported to heaven.

We live in the time prophesied by Scripture when men's hearts would fail them for fear (Luke 21:26). But for the Christian, even death is teeming with hope. "So when this corruptible has put on incorruption, and this mortal has put on immortality, then shall be brought to pass the saying that is written: Death is swallowed up in victory. O Death, where is your sting? Hades, where is your victory? The sting of death is sin, and the strength of sin is the law. But thanks be to God, who gives us the victory through our Lord Jesus Christ" (1 Cor. 15:54-57).

In a paranoid world we can live and die with confidence. Jesus has taken the sting out of death.

There's another sting that sometimes inflicts more pain than death itself. Is there any justice — any relief — when you're misunderstood?

8

Vindicated at Last!

. . . and your Father who sees in secret will reward your openly (Matt. 6:4).

One does not walk very far with Jesus before being misunderstood. Often those dearest to us are most prone to question. I heard a noted minister say, "I've been maligned, slandered, libeled, cursed — and that's just by my brothers!"

Many Christians could identify with him. Out of the hurt of such rejection, it is natural to attempt defense and vindication. So often, any self-defense only muddies the waters. Others may take the reaction of the maligned party as an implication of her guilt. Yet we live in a time when striking back is the name of the game. "I don't get mad, I get even," seems to be the slogan that many injured believers claim.

But this vindictiveness, even when one is sorely wronged or misjudged, may say more about the victim than the assailant. This era of countersuits, getting even, and mutual assured destruction ("If you hurt me, I'll bury you"), even among notable Christians, is very foreign to the spirit of Jesus. This jockeying for position and an "eye for an eye" mentality is, at best, an Old Covenant allowance and, at worst, unholy fire fueled by demons.

When Jesus was falsely accused, He did not open His mouth in rebuttal. Graphically, the Bible says He was led as a lamb to the slaughter (Isa. 53:7). It also says: "Christ suffered for you, leaving you an example, that you should follow in his steps. 'He committed no sin, and no deceit was found in his mouth.' When they hurled their insults at him, he did not retaliate; when he suffered, he made no threats. Instead, he entrusted himself to him who judges justly" (1 Pet. 2:21-23;NIV).

> *It is this decision to entrust ourselves to God for His ultimate vindication that enables believers to endure the blasts of the present.*

Our model for endurance is Jesus. Amidst the most vicious verbal and physical abuse, He endured patiently. What gave Him such strength? He saw another world and final vindication by His Father.

Do you "see" with spiritual eyes that world to come, and heaven's holy hosts that even now are watching your performance here? Look at this Scripture: "Therefore we also, since we are surrounded by so great a cloud of witnesses, let us lay aside every weight, and the sin which so easily ensnares us, and let us run with endurance the race that is set before us, looking unto Jesus, the author and finisher of our faith, who for the joy that was set before Him endured the cross, despising the shame, and has sat down at the right hand of the throne of God. For consider Him who endured such hostility from sinners against Himself, lest you become weary and discouraged in your souls" (Heb. 12:1-3).

When we are accosted while living honorably, it is easy to want to throw in the towel. After all, such attacks are unfair, unwarranted. But, at those times of discouragement and emotional injury, look to Jesus. And look ahead to your coming reward. When people libel and slander you because of your faith, great is your reward in heaven. Endurance to keep running, not paying attention to distractions, comes from trusting God to vindicate you in the end.

Life's Few "Musts"

Over the triple doorways of the magnificent Cathedral of Milan there are three inscriptions spanning the ornate arches. In one arch is carved a wreath of roses and the legend, "All that which pleases is but for a moment." In the other is carved a cross, and the words, "All that which troubles is but for a moment." But in the arch over the great central entrance to the main aisle is the inscription, "That only is important which is eternal."

What a sermon! Our pleasures are momentary. So are our trials. What matters is what is eternal. The accusations will come and go. Time heals many wounds. Circumstances change constantly. But we are moving toward an eternal world and an eternal God. The desire should be paramount with us, then, to spend our energies on eternal pursuits.

There are very few things in life that must occur. Those few "musts," however, are extremely important. Here are three.

First, if you are going to heaven at all, you *must* be born again. You must experience the inner, spiritual rebirth through faith in Christ that qualifies you for citizenship in heaven (see John 3:1-21).

The gospel invitation is to "whoever desires" (Rev. 22:17). No one comes to Christ against his will. The offer of salvation is completely optional. Once you come to Christ, however, the picture changes. You're in the army now — the Lord's army, and here is the second "must." The draft is voluntary, but once inducted, you *must* obey the requirements of the army. For instance, Christ's Great Commission to go and preach the gospel to the whole world isn't a casual suggestion. It's a mandate for the body of Christ.

And third, after your heavenly credentials are established, there is an appointment for you that is not optional. You *must* stand before the Judgment Seat of Christ (see 2 Cor. 5:10). This will be for the purpose of giving an account of your post-conversion life. It will also be the time when rewards for qualifying Christians are meted out. In light of this coming event in which the heart's secrets will be exposed, and from which there is no escape, it is incumbent upon us to live in light of this "must." Let's take a closer look at this appointment in heaven that will be based on our lives here on earth.

A Fresh Call to Holiness

Since we will stand before a perfectly holy God, we must prepare our hearts in holiness. The very word holiness has fallen on hard times these days. Even some Christians mock the popular idea of "holiness," complete with its hypocrisy and holier-than-thou-ism.

But this is a distorted perception. Biblical holiness is light years removed from self-righteousness. Self-righteousness is just that, supposed goodness that is induced by one's own self. The biblical understanding of both righteousness and holiness is that they are produced and sustained by God alone. This is one of the unique features of the Christian faith. All other major religions are primarily an attempt on man's part to induce proper living and thus be accepted by some deity. But "in the gospel a righteousness from God is revealed, a righteousness that is by faith from first to last, just as it is written: 'The righteous will live by faith' " (Rom. 1:17;NIV).

The very life of God is implanted in us by the new birth Jesus spoke of. This life is nurtured by obedience to the promptings of God's indwelling Spirit. Increased obedience produces increased sensitivity to sin. And this is the great need of our day. Our generation has become drugged and desensitized to sin and its effects.

What then is the antidote? A megadose of genuine holiness. And this is not merely for the mystics or the self-styled spiritual. It is for all who belong to Christ. There is a rather small segment of Christendom that is referred to as "the holiness movement." Actually, the entire body of Christ should be the holiness movement!

I was appalled to hear the story of a professing Christian teenager recently. His girlfriend had found out that she was pregnant. With no thought of the moral consequences, they determined to take what seemed the easiest course; she would have an abortion. As they were driving to the abortion clinic, the young man saw a stray dog with a broken leg. Immediately he stopped his car and, with a heart full of compassion for the lame animal, took the dog to the veterinarian, paying all expenses. Then he personally nursed the dog back to health.

Dear God, what has happened to us? This young man's conscience was highly sensitized to the plight of a stray dog but he was about to murder his own baby! It is past time for a moral revolution.

We do not know when death or Christ's coming will call us to account. But we do know it will happen. We can prepare now by sensitizing our hearts. These words were written in the flyleaf of my father's Bible: "This book will keep you from sin or sin will keep you from this book." There is no middle ground. And the time to face it is now.

The Final Court of Appeal

The understanding that we will stand before the Lord is certainly an impetus to holiness. But it is also a prod to steadiness and patience. For on that day, the scales will be balanced forever. Then the false accusations will be seen for what they were. Then our true motives will be exposed. And the multitudes who suffered in silence will be publicly honored. The honorable Christians who chose, like their Lord, to stay silent while their lives and characters were unjustly impugned will be vindicated at last.

9

A Sure Reward

By faith Moses, when he had grown up, refused to be known as the son of Pharaoh's daughter. He chose to be mistreated along with the people of God rather than to enjoy the pleasures of sin for a short time. He regarded disgrace for the sake of Christ as of greater value than the treasures of Egypt, because he was looking ahead to his reward (Heb. 11:24-26).

Albert Einstein was one of the great geniuses of the twentieth century. Among other accomplishments, his work helped produce the data necessary for splitting the atom. He also realized the potential for destruction that such a discovery held. One starlit night Professor Einstein was walking across the Princeton promenade with some of his students. He stopped for a moment and gazed into the starry heavens. He sighed and said, "Anyway, *that* the atom cannot destroy."

There are some things that will abide, come what may. The universe is permanent. It is the dwelling of the eternal

God. "Thus says the Lord: 'Heaven is My throne, and earth is My footstool' " (Isa. 66:1). The word of God also transcends time. "Forever, O Lord, Your word is settled in heaven" (Ps. 119:89). And the blessings with which heaven will one day reward the faithful are also permanent.

> *The wise course of action, therefore, is to pursue the permanent, to seek that which is so strong and lasting that corrosion cannot devalue it and thieves cannot displace it. This life's treasures often die a sudden, premature death.*

Acclaim is fleeting. Riches, as we've already observed, take wings and fly away. Virility and charm can vanish at the merciless hands of disease. Only the treasures of the afterlife live on.

Rewards for Service

In the parable of the talents, the master commends the faithful servant with these words: "Well done, good and faithful servant; you were faithful over a few things, I will make you ruler over many things. Enter into the joy of your Lord" (Matt. 25:21). In this statement, two strong motives emerge. The first is affirmation. There is immense power in desiring accolades from someone we love or esteem. To hear Jesus say, "Well done" — what a driving motivation! Then there is the motive of increased influence and blessing: "I will make you ruler over many things." Hope of gain for one's effective service is a potent stimulus.

Not only do two motives emerge from this passage; two qualifications surface as well. The first is simple goodness. The affirmed servant must be a good servant. No doubt this means that he is good at what he does; he is a good servant. But surely it also implies that the servant himself is good. This carries the idea of a pure heart, not motivated by a usurping lust for power. With the Psalmist he could say, "Lord, my heart is not haughty, nor my eyes lofty. Neither do I concern myself with great matters, nor with things too profound for me" (Ps. 131:1). In other words, he knows his niche and functions effectively in it. As we said a few years ago, he is willing to bloom where he is planted.

The good servant is also faithful. He's not looking for promotion from some outside source. He has a personal commitment to his master and fully intends to serve him the rest of his life. He is faithful to his task and faithful to his master, year in and year out. He doesn't chronically call in sick. He doesn't scheme ways to get out of work. He's just there, on the job.

We can quickly see that such a worker is in short supply in today's world. Companies lose millions of dollars because of employee laziness and disloyalty. We talk much today about the crying need for leadership. And, certainly, there is a great need. But, especially in the Church world, if there is a crying need for leaders, there is a bellowing need for good and faithful servants.

But what produces these qualities in servants? Without question, it is love for the master. The servant seeks to please his master because he loves him. Just so, something in the deepest part of a true believer longs to be pleasing to Jesus. "We love Him because He first loved us" (1 John 4:19). Thus, when a Christian sins, he not only grieves the Holy Spirit, he grieves himself. Yes, it is possible for a Christian to sin. But it is impossible for him to sin without remorse. Love for our Master, though His ways seem sometimes strange and difficult, produces the side effects of goodness and faithfulness.

This becomes important when we call believers to sacrificial service. As one veteran missionary said, "The need can get you there but only the love of Christ can keep you there." If we recruit with any motivation other than

Christ's love, we are liable to have those who go out in a tide of emotion get backwashed in a sea of disillusionment.

The love of Christ is a higher, more noble motivation for service than the potential of rewards. This does not mean, however, that we are to dismiss rewards as a legitimate stimulus to faithfulness. The Scriptures are replete with the principle of rewards. Hebrews 11:6 says that God is a "rewarder of those who diligently seek Him." Quite simply, we should value heaven's rewards because they are deemed valuable by Jesus. We may be assured that Jesus would not offer us anything that was not infinitely beyond price.

Down to Business

The Bible speaks of several different types of rewards in the afterlife. Usually, there are very clear guidelines prescribed for attaining these rewards. It should be remembered that heaven itself is *not* a reward; it is a gift of God's grace. It is bestowed freely on all who turn from their sins and commit their lives to Christ. "Not by works of righteousness which we have done, but according to His mercy He saved us, through the washing of regeneration and renewing of the Holy Spirit" (Titus 3:5). But rewards are just that, rewards, or, if you will, awards for meeting biblical qualifications.

First, Scripture speaks of rewards for good deeds and costly service to the Lord. For instance, winning people to Christ and turning many to a God-honoring life carries intrinsic, immediate blessings. But they also produce vast benefits in heaven. "Those who are wise shall shine like the brightness of the firmament, and those who turn many to righteousness like the stars forever and ever" (Dan. 12:3).

Also, helping the poor out of one's own need produces heavenly treasure. "Sell what you have and give alms; provide yourselves money bags which do not grow old, a treasure in the heavens that does not fail . . ." (Luke 12:33).

Then there is the promise that those who faithfully serve masters, or in our case employers, will be rewarded.

Christians are enjoined to give at all times "not with eyeservice, as menpleasers, but as servants of Christ, doing the will of God from the heart, with good will doing service, as to the Lord, and not to men, knowing that whatever good anyone does, he will receive the same from the Lord . . ." (Eph. 6:6-8).

Not to be forgotten is the ministry of hospitality, especially as it affects receiving ministers (prophets) and godly people (see Matt. 10:41; 1 Pet. 4:9). The hospitable believer will share in their reward. Further Jesus said, "Whoever gives one of these little ones only a cup of cold water in the name of a disciple, assuredly, I say to you, he shall by no means lose his reward" (Matt. 10:42).

Then the Bible says there are rewards in the afterlife for sufferings in this one. Although this is alien to much contemporary teaching, the bruised Christian rejoices that it is true. Peter reminds us, "Beloved, do not think it strange concerning the fiery trial which is to try you, as though some strange thing happened to you; but rejoice to the extent that you partake of Christ's sufferings, that when His glory is revealed, you may also be glad with exceeding joy" (1 Pet. 4:12-13). With all the teaching that trials suggest a lack of faith, difficulties could well be considered a "strange thing." But the Bible says to expect them and profit from them. When persecutions come, Jesus said to "rejoice and be exceedingly glad, for great is your reward in heaven" (Matt. 5:11-12).

Scripture also teaches that we will be rewarded in kind for our life of giving. Mercy given will reap mercy extended. "Blessed are the merciful, for they shall obtain mercy" (Matt. 5:7).

Purity of life produces a vessel of honor, set apart for a specific use. Humility and a servant's heart qualify one for greatness in the kingdom of heaven. "Therefore whoever humbles himself as this little child is the greatest in the kingdom of heaven" (Matt. 18:4).

Increased authority is awarded in response to faithfulness in the present assignment. "You were faithful over a few things, I will make you ruler over many things" (Matt. 25:21).

From these passages and the entire tone of the Bible, it is obvious that God rewards those who pursue His favor. "He is a rewarder of those who diligently seek Him" (Heb. 11:6). To be indifferent to His offer of rewards is to despise His character. God is a giver.

That Which Costs

Since God has given us His best in Jesus Christ, it naturally follows that we should give Him our best. Yet, too often only the leftovers are given to Him. One of the tragedies of much of contemporary Christianity is that our best hours, our finest efforts, the vast majority of our money, any influence we may have — these are often expended on selfish pursuits. Whatever is left, if anything, is then piously offered to God with the suggestion that He ought to be really happy He's getting anything. Such an attitude, if not blasphemous, is certainly unworthy of the majestic God who rules heaven and earth.

After David's disobedience to God's command, he prepared to make an offering to God. David had sinned against the Lord by numbering the people — looking at size and the strength of numbers. God had judged David's disobedience by sending a plague that wiped out 70,000 men. David, now fully penitent, had found a suitable place to build an altar — on the threshing floor owned by Araunah. Araunah, as a subject of King David, graciously offered to give the property to his king at no price. David's classic answer mirrors a heart of costly commitment: "No, but I will surely buy it from you for a price; nor will I offer burnt offerings to the Lord my God with that which costs me nothing" (2 Sam. 24:24).

Do our offerings to God cost us something? Sometimes our "offerings" may be no more than a token assuaging of guilt. For some, giving to God has its limits — when it hurts. But David gave something of value. That which is precious to us is to be given to Him. But here again, God is a giver. For our precious gifts offered to Him will be returned with *His* precious gifts.

There is no such thing in athletics as training for glory without suffering. Yet, amazingly, many Christians seem to think they will be "carried to the skies on flowery beds of ease." We must understand that anything that's worth anything costs something. In a statement almost completely foreign to our laid-back style of faith, the Scriptures say that Moses *chose to suffer affliction* with the people of God than to enjoy the temporary pleasures of sin. Why did He do it? What would possess a person to disdain immediate gratification and choose to suffer?

The answer is twofold. First, he realized that sin's pleasures were all too temporary. The gratification would have been only for a short season. The "stolen fruit" that is sweet to the taste sours almost immediately in the stomach. Second, Moses was allowed to see into the era of a New Covenant and esteemed "the reproach of Christ greater riches than the treasures in Egypt; for he looked to the reward" (Heb. 11:26). Moses was challenged by looking for a coming reward.

Unnamed heroes "were tortured, not accepting deliverance, that they might obtain a better resurrection" (Heb. 11:35). We speak often of faith for deliverance. But what immaculate faith is this that forgoes present deliverance in lieu of a more honored position millennia in the future!

Then there is Jesus himself, "who for the joy that was set before Him endured the cross, despising the shame, and has sat down at the right hand of the throne of God" (Heb. 12:2).

These all gave costly sacrifices to God. Why? They all saw with keener than normal perception a "joy that was set before them." Can you see it, too? These heavenly incentives for earthly living buoy us against sinking in despair. There's a bright tomorrow for those who give that which costs.

Universal Laws

The hope of lasting rewards is predicated on two "givens," two immutable principles that have been bred into the scheme of things by God. The first is that *those who humble themselves before God will be exalted by Him.* Because of its very nature, one may not be able to detect whether or not he possesses true humility, but a continual humbling of the soul before God is certainly a step in that direction. It is arrogance and self-sufficiency that bait us for the devil's trap.

It is battle enough to be opposed by Satan. It is quite another thing, however, to be opposed by God Almighty in work we may attempt for Him in an attitude of pride. That battle cannot and should not be won. That is why Scripture urges us to "be submissive to one another, and be clothed with humility, for 'God resists the proud, but gives grace to the humble.' Therefore humble yourselves under the mighty hand of God, that He may exalt you in due time" (1 Pet. 5:5-6).

Andrew Murray said, "Man's chief care, his highest virtue, and his only happiness, now and through all eternity, is to present himself as an empty vessel in which God can dwell and manifest His power and goodness."[1]

This brings us to the second universal law. *We will reap exactly what we sow.* God's Word urges us, "Sow for yourselves righteousness; reap in mercy; break up your fallow ground, for it is time to seek the Lord, till He comes and rains righteousness on you" (Hos. 10:12).

Many today seem to be sowing to the flesh and praying for a crop failure. Yet Scripture is clear. "Do not be deceived, God is not mocked; for whatever a man sows, that he will also reap. For he who sows to his flesh will of the flesh reap corruption, but he who sows to the Spirit will of the

Spirit reap everlasting life. And let us not grow weary while doing good, for in due season we shall reap if we do not lose heart" (Gal. 6:7-9).

To some extent, the "due season" is in this life. But the full crop of righteousness sown is reaped in the afterlife. Keep sowing. Your "due season" will come. And like the faithful servants, you will "enter into the joy of your Lord."

10

Treasures in Heaven

Do not lay up for yourselves treasures on earth, where moth and rust destroy and where thieves break in and steal; but lay up for yourselves treasures in heaven, where neither moth nor rust destroys and where thieves do not break in and steal. For where your treasure is, there your heart will be also (Matt. 6:19-20).

In an ancient Greek fable, the swift-footed Atlanta, confident of her success, challenged everyone to race her. Finally, Hippomenes accepted her challenge and the race began.

As expected, Atlanta took an early and commanding lead. But then Hippomenes did something completely unexpected. Taking a beautiful golden apple from his pocket, he tossed it alongside Atlanta's path as she ran. Immediately Atlanta was distracted as the apple shimmered in the sun, and Hippomenes took the lead. Soon Atlanta remembered the race, and, dropping the apple, retook the lead.

But, wait. Once again Hippomenes dropped a golden

apple at Atlanta's feet. Once again she was distracted and lost her lead, only to recover it again.

Then they were stretching toward the finish. The end of the race was in sight. A third and final time Hippomenes tossed out a beautiful apple. This time Atlanta's roving eye was her undoing. Sidetracked by the beauty, she paused. But this time, because of her closeness to the finish, she never retook the lead. Hippomenes, by his craftiness, won the race.

This is an apt description of how our cunning adversary, the devil, pitches charming distractions in our paths to slow and even stop us. A fundamental rule of racing is never look back and never look around. Always keep your eyes on the goal. The attractive fruit of the lust of the flesh, the lust of the eyes, and the pride of life may try to allure us from attention to the race. But if our eyes are fixed on Jesus Christ, their charm dims in comparison to Him.

That Day

> *Martin Luther remarked that there were only two days of importance on his calendar: Today and That Day. It's true, today is the only time we have to prepare for That Day. And it is That Day that gives full meaning to today.*

One of Karl Marx's violent objections to Christianity as he perceived it was that Christians seemed to scare people into servility by warning of a coming day of judgment. To use his words, "Religion . . . is the opiate of the people." It is true that this great coming event can be misrepresented. Yet That Day, the day of Christ's dominion and the vindication of the saints, is threaded throughout Scripture. The Bible teaches that it will come swiftly, as a thief in the night (see 2 Peter 3:10). Scripture indicates that this "great and notable day of the Lord" will coincide with a worldwide outpouring of God's Spirit, unusual phenomena in the heavens, and the return of Jesus Christ to this planet (see Acts 2:18-21).

Scripture refers to this cataclysmic day with several terms, such as the Great Day, The Day of the Lord, The Day of Christ, and the Day of God. In each reference the point is clear: While *this day* may belong to man, *That Day* belongs to God. He will have the last word on the destiny of the human race.

It seems ironic to me that many non-Christians choose Easter as their annual time to give God a tip of the hat. On Easter Sunday they forego their usual Sunday morning routine to go to church and celebrate the resurrection of Jesus Christ. Yet it is the very fact of Christ's resurrection that assures coming judgment on a day already appointed by God — That Day. God "now commands all men everywhere to repent, because He has appointed a day on which He will judge the world in righteousness by the man whom He has ordained. He has given assurance of this to all by raising Him from the dead" (Acts 17:30-31).

A man was once asked by a friend his beliefs concerning the return of Christ and the kingdom of God. He responded, "I'm a pan-millennialist."

"Whatever in the world is that?" his friend inquired.

"That means I believe it will all pan out in the end."

Whatever one's millennial position, there are certain verities concerning That Day on which all Bible-believing Christians can agree.

First, Scripture declares That Day to be a day of *revelation*. Secrets tucked away securely in hearts will be disclosed. For the person living for the Lord, this is not a threat but a hope. He looks to the day when his true motives will be exposed.

In light of this coming disclosure, the believer should forego judgment on even his own motives as well as the motives of others. While we are to allow the Holy Spirit to examine our hearts continually, at the same time we should guard against an unhealthy, constant introspection.

A little boy with a small carrot patch complained to his mother that his carrots weren't growing. "What's the matter, dear?" his mother asked. "Are you keeping the weeds pulled and giving your carrots enough water?"

"Oh, yes, Mother," the lad replied. "Not only that, I pull up my carrots every day to see if they're growing."

Often we pull up sprouting growth with well-intentioned introspection. We should be willing to just let growth happen, nourished by the vine life of Jesus Christ and the living water of the Holy Spirit.

The apostle Paul acknowledged criticism of his ministry but deemed it "a very small thing" (see 1 Cor. 4:3). Further, he refrained from self-judgment; all such determinations are obviously subjective and therefore faulty. We will either grade ourselves too high or too low. Paul was content to forego judgment on his life, by himself or others. Rather, he would wait for the Lord's final assessment.

Second, That Day is a day of *retribution.* The scales will be forever balanced. The inequities will be forever dissolved.

Paul was physically whipped by Pharisees and verbally whipped by some Christians. Even some churches he was instrumental in founding later questioned the validity of his ministry. After facing tribunals with predetermined thoughts against him, Paul looked forward to facing a righteous Judge whose only vested interest is in those He has redeemed. The Apostle anticipated a reward for his faithfulness, "which the Lord, the righteous Judge, will give to me on that Day" (2 Tim. 4:8).

Third, That Day will be a day of *reigning* for Jesus Christ. John the Revelator says he was "in the Spirit on the Lord's Day" (Rev. 1:10). Many Bible scholars believe this is not a reference to the Sabbath but to that coming day when

Jesus reigns supreme. It was during this vision, on the Lord's Day, that Jesus Christ was revealed to John in almost indescribable splendor. Although this is Spirit-inspired Scripture, one senses that John is groping for words in our limited human vocabulary to describe the reigning King. "His head and His hair were white like wool, as white as snow, and His eyes like a flame of fire; His feet were like fine brass, as if refined in a furnace, and His voice as the sound of many waters; He had in His right hand seven stars, out of His mouth went a sharp two-edged sword, and His countenance was like the sun shining in its strength. And when I saw Him, I fell at His feet as dead" (Rev. 1:14-17).

That Day will be His day. Forever gone will be the mockings and jeerings against Him. The Lamb has now returned as a Lion. The Lord Jesus will be "... revealed from heaven with His mighty angels, in flaming fire taking vengeance on those who do not know God, and on those who do not obey the gospel of our Lord Jesus Christ. These shall be punished with everlasting destruction from the presence of the Lord and from the glory of His power, when He comes, in that Day, to be glorified in His saints and to be admired among all those who believe" (2 Thess. 1:7-10).

Coronation Day

That Day is not only our coronation day, most importantly, it is His. Jesus Christ will be glorified in His saints. And believers will begin their rule with Him. Here we talk of long-term and short-term investments. With heaven's rewards in mind, it is always sound to make spiritual long-term investments. The interest accrued on the principal is out of this world!

It is always in our best interest to condition ourselves to God-honoring living. And we should be just as dedicated in our spiritual workouts as athletes in training. For, in fact, we are in training — to rule over the nations in the coming world order. Then Jesus will reign and those who qualify will reign with Him.

When describing eternal rewards, the Bible often refers to them as crowns. Interestingly, two Greek words are translated "crown." From one we get our word *diadem*. The use of this word is always reserved as a symbol of kingly or imperial dignity. It is this royal diadem with which Jesus Christ will one day be crowned as King of kings.[1]

In contrast, the crowns of overcoming Christians are symbols of triumph. Scripture speaks of five crowns believers may win. Clear qualifications are given for each crown. To win these crowns is to have treasures in heaven. So living in such a way as to secure these symbols of triumph forms basic motivation for living an overcoming life.

The *crown of righteousness* is reserved for those who so love the thought of Jesus' return that they have reordered their lives in view of His coming. This beautiful victor's garland is for those who have experienced the purifying effect of the imminent return of Christ.

When I was a boy my mother had a foolproof way of correcting my bad behavior. All she had to do was remind me, "Your father is coming soon." Believe me, it had a purifying effect! Just so, the prospect of the return of Christ at any moment has a sanctifying effect on the Christian's life. The blessed hope of Christ's imminent return is a purgative in our lives: "And everyone who has this hope in Him purifies himself, just as He is pure" (1 John 3:3).

Too often we have used the message of the second coming of Christ primarily as an evangelistic warning to non-Christians. But the essential message unbelievers must hear is of Christ's *first* coming, the biblical *kerygma* of His death on their behalf, and His resurrection. The message of Christ's second coming is the blessed hope of the believer. And it is contemplation of this glorious event that purifies and thus qualifies the believer to receive the crown of righteousness. As Paul approached the end of this life, he rejoiced: "I have fought the good fight, I have finished the race, I have kept the faith. Finally, there is laid up for me the crown of righteousness, which the Lord, the righteous

Judge, will give me on that Day, and not to me only but also to all who have loved His appearing" (2 Tim. 4:7-8).

It should be remembered that love for Christ is the highest motive for serving Him. Most of us, however, find that our motives are not fully sanctified at all times. For those of us still in the process of being changed from glory to glory, it doesn't hurt to remember that Christ could come at any time. And certainly we want to be found serving Him with integrity when He comes. "Who then is that faithful and wise steward, whom his master will make ruler over his household . . . ? Blessed is that servant whom his master will find so doing when he comes. Truly, I say to you that he will make him ruler over all that he has" (Luke 12:42-44). The scope of our future stewardship is determined by our faithfulness now. And our desire for faithfulness is prodded by the knowledge that this may be the day He returns.

With every day we draw closer to the time when Jesus will split the skies. Yet, ironically, we seem to be hearing less about this wonderful, blessed hope. Some Christians seem content to set up an earthly kingdom that can exist equally well with or without the physical return of Christ. But this has not been the historic longing of the Church. Yes, Christians have always longed for Christ's kingdom to come. But historically they have always tied the coming of the Kingdom with the coming of the King.

There were dual thrills that ran concurrently through the hearts of the early believers. Any careful study of Scripture shows that the Early Church expected the physical return of Christ from heaven any day. Yet, at the same time, they made long-term plans on how to get the gospel to the farthest reaches of their known world. They were planting the Kingdom while waiting for the Rapture.

Why do we tend to see these two hopes as dichotomous? Is it because we, unlike the Early Church, have had 20 centuries to systematize our theology? Have we polarized hopes that God would have us view as a unified whole?

In any event, a righteous life is always in order for those who call themselves Christians. And the crown of righteousness awaits those who long for Christ's return — and live like it.

The qualification of the *crown of life* is to be faithful until death. "Do not fear any of those things which you are about to suffer," Jesus urged the church in Smyrna. "Be faithful until death, and I will give you the crown of life" (Rev. 2:10). He encourages His church today with the same offer. This victorious crown of life is reserved for those who serve the Lord well through suffering. Often called the martyr's crown, it is also laid in store for those who give their last full sacrifice of devotion in furthering the gospel. Some observers speculate that more than 200,000 Christians worldwide may be killed for their witness in the next few years. For each of them, there is a victor's crown of life on the other side of their suffering.

There is no hope of rectifying the injustices that have assaulted suffering saints from the perspective of this life alone. From the limited perspective of the present, everything doesn't always add up and good is not always rewarded in kind. It will take the judgment seat of Christ to properly honor war-scarred saints who have faithfully lived for Christ and seemingly received only more difficulties in this life as a result.

James encourages such faithful soldiers, "Blessed is the man who endures temptation; for when he has been proved, he will receive the crown of life which the Lord has promised to those who love Him" (James 1:12). Here the thought is carried beyond actual martyrdom. To die to self, whether this is expressed in physical death or other courageous sacrifice, qualifies one to receive this crown. James also describes the essence of what it really means to love Jesus. To love Jesus is to endure when we are tempted. In this verse he gives a spiritual postulate: A = B and B = A. The person who loves Christ is the one who endures temptation and *vice versa.* Devotion under attack — that's the test of love's commitment.

The *incorruptible crown* is conferred on those who live disciplined lives as good soldiers of Jesus Christ. It is the heavenly, imperishable laurel given to winners in the greatest race of all — this race that is set before us as believers. The writer to the Hebrews reminds us that heaven's grandstands are filled with saintly spectators who cheer us on in the contest (see Heb. 12:1). Since they are watching and, more importantly, since He is watching, we run with perseverance.

To win in this race we must be properly trained. And life sees to it that we go through spiritual drills far more grueling than leg lifts and wind sprints. As with an athlete in training, we may be called upon to forego even legitimate desires for a time to train as spiritual champions. Yet there can be no true discipleship to Jesus without discipline. To put it bluntly, there are two pains that are set before the believer. There is the pain of denying the control of the Holy Spirit and living for the flesh. And there is the pain of denying the flesh and living under the control of the Holy Spirit. One pain produces nothing but regret and a destroyed life. The other pain produces an incorruptible crown.

The body's desires for food, rest, and sex, for instance, are implanted by God. An illicit acquiescence to any of these needs, however, constitutes idolatry. We must bring even the legitimate needs of the body under discipline, just as an athlete does who trains for the big event. "Everyone who competes in the games goes into strict training. They do it to get a crown that will not last; but we do it to get a crown that will last forever" (1 Cor. 9:25;NIV).

The *crown of rejoicing* is fittingly named. This is the soul winner's crown. It will be bestowed on those who love the lost and prayerfully win them to Christ by the example of their lives and by their verbal witness.

Every believer carries the evangelistic mandate. All

Christians should live in light of the Great Commission given by our commander in chief. His command to go and make disciples of all the nations is incumbent upon all who have experienced a spiritual rebirth. Under this command the Lord's army is placed into two groups: those few who are gifted as evangelists, and the vast majority who are to "do the work of an evangelist" (2 Tim. 4:5). Into whichever category we may fall, the command is the same for all. We are ordered as believers to open our mouths and share the Good News of Jesus Christ.

One day in an evangelism class in seminary, we were discussing the reasons behind a certain denomination's drop in number of conversions from the previous year. Both the professor and students postulated reasons ranging from the rise in the national median age to poor weather. Finally, I felt I must speak. My hand went up slowly. (That hand of question got me into a lot of "discussions" during those years.) "While all of these may be factors," I said, "I don't think any of them is the real reason why more people aren't being converted."

"Well, David," the professor queried, "just what do you think *is* the reason?"

"Sir," I began, "I don't wish to appear flippant or judgmental. But the Bible says that when Zion travails she brings forth children."

It's true both spiritually and physically. Breathing exercises and prenatal classes notwithstanding, pain precedes physical birth. Just so, somebody has to be burdened before children are born into the Kingdom. That's why the soul winner's crown is a crown of rejoicing: you have to do some weeping to get it. "He who continually goes forth weeping, bearing seed for sowing, shall doubtless come again with rejoicing, bringing his sheaves with him" (Ps. 126:6).

Those who take this supreme command of our Lord seriously will, of course, obey it. And for those who are obedient a crown of rejoicing is reserved. Often in this life the Christian witness will bear a tearful burden for the unsaved. According to God's promise, "Those who sow in tears shall reap in joy" (Ps. 126:5).

I cannot conceive of anything more joyful in the universe than the sight of others in heaven whom we have won to Christ. It will be just as Paul said: "For what is our hope, or joy, or crown of rejoicing? Is it not even you in the presence of our Lord Jesus Christ at His coming? For you are glory and joy" (1 Thess. 2:19-20).

May I ask you a pointed question? Will anyone be eternally grateful to you for your witness to them? Will anyone approach you in heaven and say, "I'm here because of you. Your love, prayers, and witness brought me to Christ"?

Finally, the *crown of glory* awaits those who have faithfully pastored and shepherded the people of God. It will be for those who feed the flock of God with prayerful diligence. The indiscretions of a few spotlighted ministers tend to discredit all ministers. This is a terrible and false indictment on many godly people who serve Christ nobly and without fanfare day in and day out. So this crown extends, in my opinion, to those who lift up the hands of their leaders in love, affirmation, and support. Jesus said, "He who receives a prophet in the name of a prophet shall receive a prophet's reward" (Matt. 10:41).

Peter describes the pastoral qualifications for this laurel of victory. "To the elders among you, I appeal as a fellow elder, a witness of Christ's sufferings and one who also will share in the glory to be revealed: Be shepherds of God's flock that is under your care, serving as overseers — not because you must, but because you are willing, as God wants you to be; not greedy for money, but eager to serve; not lording it over those entrusted to you, but being examples to the flock. And when the Chief Shepherd appears, you will receive the crown of glory that will never fade away" (1 Pet. 5:1-4;NIV).

Many faithful ministers serve in situations that appear totally unsuccessful to natural eyes. Many serve diligently in obscure settings with seemingly little influence. But when Christ returns, these faithful "no-name" servants will be thrust into universal prominence. As the redeemed of all ages look on, the King of kings will confer His approval on them in the form of a crown of glory.

Crown Him with Many Crowns

The purpose of these crowns is not, of course, to flaunt them. They will be symbols of victorious service in the previous sphere. They will also serve as something tangible we can lay at the feet of Jesus. True worship always involves giving. And nothing could be more thrilling than to have something in our hands of high value (as heaven measures worth) to offer in worship before our King.

The Tower of London is the secure deposit for the priceless Crown Jewels of England. The dazzling brilliance of these regal crowns is breathtaking. The Queen's coronation crown alone contains 2,738 diamonds, 277 pearls, 18 sapphires, 11 emeralds, and 5 rubies.

Yet, as awe-inspiring as these regal crowns are, they cannot be favorably compared to the immeasurable beauty and worth of heaven's treasures. "Eye has not seen, nor ear heard, nor have entered into the heart of man the things which God has prepared for those who love Him" (1 Cor. 2:9).

— 11 —

Beware! Jewel Thieves at Work

Let us hold fast the confession of our hope without wavering, for He who promised is faithful (Heb. 10:23).

A friend of mine told me a tragic story. One night as he was driving home, he saw a house on fire. Firemen were just arriving and seemed helpless to prevent the home's rapid destruction to ash and cinder.

Across the street was the elderly couple who had lived in the home. My friend went over to offer words of encouragement. As he drew closer he saw the wife rocking in a rocking chair staring blankly at the licking flames. Behind her stood her traumatized husband, patting her on the shoulder, with the same frozen gaze of fear.

You see, the loss of the house was the least of their worries. It seems this couple didn't believe in banks. Over their 40 years of marriage they had stashed away every spare dollar in a secret place in their home, "for a rainy day." What they did not count on was a night of fire. Their entire life's savings rose in worthless incense toward the sky.

Up in Smoke

As has already been stated, the Christian who lives to please himself jeopardizes any hope of treasures in heaven. He runs the risk of seeing his life go up in smoke when he stands before the Lord.

Remember, the judgment seat of Christ is not to determine whether or not we will be in heaven. Thank God, we will already be there because of our faith in Jesus Christ. When we stand before the Lord, it will not be in judgment of our sins. Our sins have already been judged by being placed on Christ at the cross. Our sins are forever covered by His blood. This judgment of believers is not a judgment of sins. It is a judgment of our deeds and the motives behind them. So instead of judging other Christians we had better judge our own lives in preparation for His scrutiny of our every thought, word, and deed. The fact that our sins will never be brought up against us is no license to sin. Any disobedience in our lives is deadly. The wages of sin is death for anybody, believer and unbeliever alike. Sin keeps us from serving the Lord acceptably and this inevitably means a loss of reward.

This is well illustrated in the sad story of Lot in Genesis 18 and 19. Lot's Uncle Abraham was a godly man. Lot, however, was not walking with the Lord and eventually lost his testimony even with his own family. Judgment finally came. And while Lot was spared the fire and brimstone, everything he lived for was burned up. Lot himself was saved "yet so as through fire." But he was left with nothing.

The Greek word for "judgment seat" is *bema*. It is well translated by Williams as the "tribunal of Christ." It was before the *bema* of Rome's supposed authority that Jesus was brought before Pilate. But it is before heaven's *bema* that Jesus will one day judge Pilate. It was before the *bema* in Caesarea that Paul made his defense before Felix. But it is before heaven's *bema* that Felix must make his defense to

Christ. And it is before this *bema* that our lives will be scrutinized by the Lord Jesus, not, as with Pilate and Felix, to determine our salvation, but rather to determine what rewards, if any, we will receive.

There is a clear distinction between the nature and, perhaps, even the times of the judgments of believers and unbelievers. The Great White Throne is the judgment of unbelievers (see Rev. 20:11-15). The judgment seat of Christ is the judgment of believers' work (see 2 Corinthians 5:9-10). The Great White Throne is punitive, resulting in the expulsion of the unsaved from the presence of the Lord forever. The judgment seat of Christ is remunerative, resulting in rewards for qualifying believers.

It is important for us to keep this vital doctrine of coming judgment in balance, just as Scripture does. We must not tip the scales by teaching grace to the exclusion of the believer's accountability. Nor are we at liberty to revert to any legalistic aberration of the gospel by teaching salvation through works.

Christians have always had differences of opinion concerning the permanence of salvation. I have very decided views on this subject myself. That, however, is not the subject of this book. For now we will leave it to the theologians to discuss the potential for "falling from grace" and the perseverance of the saints.

But one thing is beyond dispute. Whether or not salvation may be lost, rewards certainly can be. The ground that has been gained spiritually must be guarded tenaciously. Jesus encouraged the faithful church at Philadelphia, "Behold, I come quickly! Hold fast what you have, that no one may take your crown" (Rev. 3:11).

Crown-Snatchers

It's worth noting that Jesus says it is people, not events, that can snatch away our rewards. For, behind undesirable circumstances inevitably there are people. It is relationships, good and bad, that affect our performance in any area.

The following group of crown-snatchers is by no means exhaustive, but will show some of the results of faulty relationships that set us up for the loss of rewards.

Burnout is one early evidence of potentially lost rewards. When I first began to see this term several years ago, interestingly, it was in reference to ministers, not company executives or other emotionally high-risk professionals. And this was in secular as well as religious writings.

In my opinion, we are living in the day prophesied by Isaiah. "Even the youths shall faint and be weary, and the young men shall utterly fall" (Isa. 40:30). Bright men and women, fresh out of Bible college or seminary, enter ministry brimming with hope and vision. Within a few years (sometimes a few months) they are demoralized and beaten. One reason is because our adversary, the devil, has picked up his pace of resistance or oppression.

Another key factor in burnout among ministers is that supernatural ministry is often attempted in natural strength. Clergy and lay people alike need aid from heaven. We must remember that our strength is from God himself. "*He* gives power to the weak, and to those who have no might *He* increases strength" (Isa. 40:29). How then do we get this God-infused strength that bolsters us against burnout? Again, the answer is precise: "Those who wait on the Lord shall renew their strength; they shall mount up with wings like eagles, they shall run and not be weary, they shall walk and not faint" (Isa. 40:31).

I believe the key to longevity in service for Christ is to keep our souls happy in the Lord. George Mueller, who carried the heavy load of an orphanage and other far reaching ministries, understood this well. He said, "My first assignment every day is to get my soul happy in the Lord." Mueller accomplished this by a daily mix each morning of prayer, praise, and devotional Bible reading. In his later years he was able to say, "I'm 80 years old. I've read the Bible through 55 times. And I'm happy, happy, happy."

This great man of faith minimized his vulnerability to burnout by maintaining a clear conscience and a joyful heart.

The *trivia trap* also ensnares many today. Our proclivity for entertainment snuggles up to us and whispers that we should wait until the proverbial "tomorrow" to seek what is really important. Tonight, we need to relax. And before we know it we have relaxed our way through an entire lifetime.

Let's reorder our use of time to coincide with that which is ultimately important. And things of ultimate importance are exceedingly few. That which is genuinely vital and eternal is to glorify God, to love God, and to throw our energies into the battle to make Him glorified and loved in our generation.

Because of the pressures of modern living, many wish to insulate themselves from any further bad news. Insulating oneself from outside worries can be healthy up to a certain point. But blindness to impending disaster is not noble; it is foolish. Those who sound warnings are often labeled alarmists. But aren't "alarmists" friends, not enemies, if their warnings can prevent destruction? Remember, Paul Revere was a hero. Those who may have been temporarily angered that he roused them from slumber later thanked him for saving their lives.

If a ship were sinking, who would be more truly benevolent: the guy passing out drugs to dull the panic or the guy passing out life jackets? Even if those drowning around us are angered by our attempts, we must keep yelling out warnings to come back to the lifeboats. And we must keep tossing life preservers in their direction. We dare not get caught in the trivia trap of noninvolvement.

The twin villains of *disunity and disloyalty* are also rampant in our day. The renewal movement, which began 30 years ago in a unity perhaps unparalleled since the Reformation, is now seriously splintered. Unselfish deference devolved into ego empires.

I personally believe that the greater agenda of the Holy Spirit through the renewal may have been the spiritual reunification of the Church. This may have been of equal importance with the renewal of spiritual gifts. Of course, the unity I'm speaking of is not organizational or man-made. In fact, I believe the unity within the renewal was God's counter to much of the liberal, man-induced unity based on a compromise of the so-called ecumenical movement. God was producing a spiritual bonding, a unity that went past labels to a common commitment to Jesus as Lord.

But all of that has now been jeopardized. For with the big blessings came big bucks. And with that came power maneuvers. And the unimpeded flow of the Spirit was at least partially blocked. In 1977, 70,000 renewal-oriented Christians met in Kansas City in an astonishing display of unity and spiritual dynamism. Ten years later this same segment of Christendom met in New Orleans. While it was still wonderful, participants were reeling from the aftershocks of national scandals about prominent television evangelists and the ensuing negative press. And the New Orleans meeting, which was billed to be bigger and better than Kansas City, drew about half the crowd.

Our public disunity reveals our private disloyalties and infighting. The most heart-wrenching thing about our highly publicized shortcomings is not our moral failures. It is the vicious and often bloodthirsty spirit of exposure that has gripped ministerial rivals. Where are the noble sons who will cover the nakedness of a compromised prophet as Shem and Japhath did for Noah?

But there is one crown-snatcher that may be more deadly than any previously mentioned. It is the vicious villain of *bitterness*. Over the years I have watched this killer sideline more people than any other sin. No wonder the writer to the Hebrews pleads with his readers, "Pursue peace with all men, and holiness, without which no one will see the Lord: looking diligently lest anyone fall short of the grace of

God; lest any root of bitterness springing up cause trouble, and by this many become defiled" (Heb. 12:14-15).

Bitterness is cancerous to the spirit. If unchecked it can cancel out the good effects of years of service. I'm thinking now of several individuals who were household names among Christians 10 or 20 years ago. Today, they have become hardened, angry people, living in self-made shells of isolation. Their former joy, anointing, and influence are all vanished. Unless we deal ruthlessly with bitterness, allowing the Lord to yank it out of us by the roots, our past influence will be neutralized and our future rewards will be jeopardized. David Hubbard reminds us, "The great danger in having enemies is not what they may do to us — it is what we do to ourselves as we allow harsh, bitter, angry reactions to develop."[1]

Like Him

In contrast to succumbing to the crown-snatchers, we are to "make it our aim . . . to be well pleasing to Him" (2 Cor. 5:9). It is possible to be preserved blameless, body, soul, and spirit to the coming of Christ (see 1 Thess. 5:23). If it were not possible, Paul would not have prayed for it.

> *Even in an era when moral lapses seem to be the order of the day, God "is able to keep you from stumbling, and to present you faultless before the presence of His glory with exceeding joy"* (Jude 24).

The mystery of worship is that the worshiper becomes like the object of his worship. Just think of the millions who worship gods of wood and stone. These false deities are incapable of hearing or perceiving. And many of those entrapped in such religions become like the false gods they worship: dull, indifferent, and impotent. Then consider the millions of religious zealots who, though they worship one God, see Him only as avenging and full of wrath. Once again, the worshiper is becoming like the perception of the one worshipped.

But Bible-centered Christians are also destined to become like the object of their worship, Jesus Christ. With eyes focused on Him, we are being changed into His likeness "from glory to glory, just as by the Spirit of the Lord" (2 Cor. 3:28). We are destined to be like Him.

God has taken you on as a lifetime project. His one great objective is to conform you into the image of His Son. That is why there are no chance encounters in the life of the Christian. Each blow of life is designed to shape us more into the family likeness of Jesus Christ. "And we know that all things work together for good to those who love God, to those who are the called according to His purpose. For whom He foreknew, He also predestined to be conformed to the image of His Son" (Rom. 8:28-29).

This progressive conformity to the image of Jesus will continue until it is consummated in His return for us. When He comes, the very brilliance of His appearing will finish the process of changing us into His likeness. "Beloved, now we are children of God; and it has not yet been revealed what we shall be, but we know that when He is revealed, we shall be like Him, for we shall see Him as He is" (1 John 3:2).

Like Him! That's your future. God has determined to take off all the rough edges. And when He's finished — and He *will* finish — you will look like Jesus. "Being confident of this very thing, that He who has begun a good work in you will complete it until the day of Jesus Christ" (Phil. 1:6).

Praise, Honor, and Glory

Celestial jewel thieves and crown-snatchers notwithstanding, a fantastic future awaits every Christian. My own study of this fascinating subject of rewards convinces me that all true believers will receive affirmation from Jesus Christ when they stand before Him. This, in effect, is the minimal reward — loving affirmation from the Lord. At the same time that the counsels of the hearts are revealed, "each one's praise will come from God" (1 Cor. 4:5). Each individual believer has been born to a living hope. That hope is our inheritance in heaven. Concerning the nature of this inheritance, Peter says it is incorruptible, undefiled, and lasting (see 1 Pet. 1:3-4). And this inheritance is, even as you read, already reserved in heaven for you.

Every believer will at least receive praise from God. This is the portion of every child of God. We are urged, however, to move into further realms of rewards; namely, honor and glory. "In this you greatly rejoice, though now for a little while, if need be, you have been grieved by various trials, that the genuineness of your faith, being much more precious than gold that perishes, though it is tested by fire, may be found to praise, honor, and glory at the revelation of Jesus Christ" (1 Pet. 1:6-7). In my opinion, "praise, honor, and glory" is not a redundancy. Rather, each represents a level of heavenly rewards.

While everyone will receive praise at the judgment seat of Christ, those who have faithfully served Christ will be honored. Jesus promised as much when He said, "If anyone serves Me, him My Father will honor" (John 12:26).

But there is a higher level still. The Bible promises that those believers who have suffered for Christ will in some way receive special glory from Him. "If you are reproached for the name of Christ, blessed are you, for the Spirit of glory and of God rests upon you" (1 Pet. 4:14). No doubt we will all be surprised in heaven when we see who's at the head of the line. Then, indeed, the last shall be first. Those who have suffered and even died for Jesus Christ in obscurity will be thrust into eternal prominence. And many of today's high visibility "elite" may have to take a back seat to a new class of the uniquely glorious.

This is one reason I try always to be sensitive to the needs of Third World pastors, praying grandmothers, and suffering children, among others. The disenfranchised of this world may well make up heaven's new elite. Many of the dispossessed Christians of this age will reign with Christ and rule nations in the new order.

The law of seedtime and harvest is in effect both in this life and the afterlife. This life serves as the planting time and the future life brings harvest. The farmer must toil in planting seed if he expects a harvest. And the Christian must pay the price of service for the Lord now if he expects a harvest of rewards in eternity.

Tim LaHaye has said, "Christians are now earning their position of service for Christ during the millennium. Our most enjoyable and profitable activities on this earth involve service for Jesus Christ. In like manner our most exciting experiences in the millennial Kingdom will include administration of His program. If Christians really understood this, they would surely be motivated to pursue better and more lasting heights of Christian service."[2]

For every genuine Christian, and certainly for those who serve and suffer, the best is yet to be.

12

Seeing the Invisible

Therefore we also, since we are surrounded by so great a cloud of witnesses, let us lay aside every weight, and the sin which so easily ensnares us, and let us run with endurance the race that is set before us, looking unto Jesus, the author and finisher of our faith, who for the joy that was set before Him endured the cross, despising the shame, and has sat down at the right hand of the throne of God (Heb. 12:1-2).

William James said, "The great use of life is to spend it for something that outlasts it." This is especially true for the Christian. Unselfish service, fervent prayer, and the sacrificial giving of time and money yield immense blessing both to current and succeeding generations. To spend one's life for something that will outlast it is part of our innate longing for immortality.

Some would have us believe the act of sex is merely to satisfy physical passion. But there are far more profound reasons for procreation. Not the least of these is man's desire and inner need to continue some kind of legacy.

We acknowledge, with Scripture, that life is merely a vapor that is here for but a moment. The violence of modern civilization underscores our vulnerability to sudden death via car and plane accidents, crime, and war. Yet something within us cries for some kind of continuance, some way to influence things 50 years or even 100 years from now.

Some segments of Christianity believe that the prayer ministry of Christians continues into the afterlife. They believe that, since Christians live forever, they look down on current events and, from their heavenly vantage point, continue to pray to the Father. While this concept is controversial, all Christians agree that the prayers we pray now can affect the outcome of events yet future. We are to think, live, and pray toward the future.

The Way Everlasting

Scripture is replete with reminders that we are mere transients on our way to a more permanent city. As spiritual children of Abraham, like him, we are to look "for the city which has foundations, whose builder and maker is God" (Heb. 11:10). We are further urged to emulate the model of those who live for eternity. The self-styled existentialists who live only for the present and the material bring reproach on the name of Christ. In fact, Paul calls them enemies of the gospel. "Their destiny is destruction, their god is their stomach, and their glory is in their shame. Their mind is on earthly things. But our citizenship is in heaven" (Phil. 3:19-20;NIV). Paul urges us to "stand firm in the Lord" (Phil. 4:1;NIV).

The choice is ours: We can live for the present or we can live for the future. We can live to pamper our whims or we can invest in eternity. We are incessantly bombarded with stimuli. All around us a myriad of choices clamors for our hearts and minds. Perhaps the greatest challenge to the Christian of our day is to pull away from the maddening crowd, quiet his heart before God, and fine-tune his receptor to heaven's still, small voice.

We live in a world of loud blastings. Coupled with the pressures of modern life, these noises have spawned an outbreak of intense anxiety. Yet every age has its own set of pressures. King David, for instance, felt the burden of keeping his nation righteous before God. In the midst of intense pressure, David prayed not to lose sight of the eternal: "Lead me in the way everlasting" (Ps. 139:24). One Hebrew scholar told me this prayer could also be translated, "Lead me in the way of everlasting things."

If we are led in the way of everlasting things, we will readjust our schedules in certain areas. A life given to everlasting things will give high priority first of all to prayer. Prayer is the highest call of all. Prayer not only affects our current circumstances, but launches God's will into the future. Whether one is rich or poor, he or she can leave a legacy of prayer that will bring untold blessings to those who follow.

Prayer always precedes revival. Some are called to pray for an awakening that they will never see except from heaven's grandstands. Their prayers in the present lay the groundwork for the Spirit's outpouring in the future.

The disciples were not chosen because of advanced spirituality over previous generations. They were simply blessed to live in the fullness of time for Messiah to come. Jesus reminded them of their debt to the godly legacy of their predecessors when he said, "Many prophets and righteous men desired to see what you see, and did not see it, and to hear what you hear, and did not hear it" (Matt. 13:17).

We, too, owe an immeasurable debt to those who have gone before us. It's true that our resources are much more vast than in the past. It also seems true that we are able to accomplish things for the Lord more quickly than in the past. But this is precisely because of the godly lives and prayers of our forebearers. If we seem to be rising to previously unknown heights, it is because we are standing on the shoulders of giants.

Probably everyone who reads this book knows the name Billy Graham. But few have heard of Pearl Goode. Yet, when we get to heaven, we will likely find that a great deal of Graham's success is due to her.

You see, when Billy was a young evangelist in the early fifties, this Methodist laywoman began to hear and read that God was raising up a national evangelist. God impressed her to assist this young preacher, not so much with money but with prayer. She wrote to Graham's office in Minneapolis and requested his crusade itinerary. Then, for the next several years, unknown to anyone, she would travel to the crusade city, check into an inexpensive hotel, and lock the door. Throughout the days of the crusade she would stay in her room, praying down God's power and blessings.

A life committed to everlasting things is committed to prayer. This brings benefit both to ourselves and others. It benefits our own era and generations to come. And it conditions us to the coming reign of Jesus Christ.

A life given to everlasting things is marked, secondly, by praise. Praise is the language of heaven. And if joy is the livelihood of heaven, this joy is generated by praise and worship of a perfect Redeemer-God. The Bible says that the praise and worship of sincere believers is attractive and beautiful. There is nothing quite so moving as honest praise and worship from a pure heart.

This is a powerful evangelistic tool as well. When unbelievers see honest-hearted Christians worshipping their God, something happens to them. The reality of the gospel may grip non-Christians through observing the Church in worship more than through the most eloquent sermon.

Someone has said that the Church preaches to answer questions raised by its praise. David said, "He has put a new song in my mouth — praise to our God; many will see it and fear, and will trust in the Lord" (Ps. 40:3). Our genuine praise to God elicits conviction in the previously unconvicted. After they have seen God's glory through the power of praise, they then trust the Lord.

If someone follows the path of everlasting things, his life will be marked by prayer and praise. But such a life also has a high commitment to people. Relationships matter deeply to the eternity-oriented Christian. Very few things are eternal. According to the second law of thermodynamics the earth itself is in a state of entropy; it is winding down, dying away. What's left when the planets themselves are gone?

God remains. His Word remains. And people remain. Every person you have ever known will live forever — somewhere. His or her destiny is either eternity with Christ or eternity without Him. So we should wrap arms of love around people. We should extend evangelistic warmth and compassion to non-Christians and nonpartisan fellowship and love to fellow Christians. In his classic sermon "The Weight of Glory," C.S. Lewis reminded his hearers that they were seated next to immortal beings. If for no other reason, we should honor each other with dignity. We eat with, work with, disagree with, and live with immortal souls.

A Deeper Perception

For hundreds of years scientists viewed things on the basis of Newtonian physics. Things were as they appeared to be: fixed and verifiable with nothing beyond. But with the advent of quantum mechanics we were able to envision new possibilities. Things may not be as bolted down as we had thought. Scientists are now conceding that there may be more to something than what we see, no matter how powerful the microscope.

Elisha's servant was stricken with fear as he looked on the horizon. What he saw was enough to scare anybody: he and Elisha were surrounded by foreign armies. The prophet encouraged his servant with the incredible words that "those who are with us are more than those who are with them." But how could that possibly be? Weren't their sworn enemies breathing down their necks? But then Elisha prayed, "Lord,

I pray, open his eyes that he may see." Immediately the servant saw that the enemy army surrounding them was itself surrounded by hosts of horses and chariots of fire.

What a strange prayer, "that he may see." Didn't the servant already see? He saw well indeed, well enough to see the problem. But he did not see well enough to see the solution. He needed a deeper perception. And this new way of seeing melted his fear.[1]

In the last several years there has been a rise of interest in demons. Many self-proclaimed spiritual leaders pride themselves on the ability to perceive demons and their activities. But this is really no great achievement. Even the nearsighted servant, through no special endowment, was able to see the enemies of the Lord. They were obviously there, right in front of him.

Frankly, it takes no rare insight to realize that Satan and his hosts are poised to do battle against us. So I have a question for those who see a demon behind every bush: Do you see the *angels* behind them? Only a third of the heavenly angels fell through rebellion. They now constitute the demonic forces. But that means there are still two angels for every demon! It brings no comfort to a threatened church to announce that demons are poised to attack. What we need is better spiritual eyesight. We must see the far more numerous heavenly armies of the Lord who are even now ambushing hell's designs.

If we see the invisible we are strengthened to endure the tangible. Moses "endured as seeing Him who is invisible" (Heb. 11:27). So can we. There are three trademarks of a person with an eternal perspective; this is the first, that he or she *sees the invisible.*

Following close on the heels of heightened spiritual sight is more highly sensitized hearing. Just as dogs are keenly sensitized to pitches humans can't even hear, so the eternity-oriented believer hears what others do not. Not only does he see the invisible, he *hears the inaudible.*

Some in the media have had a heyday attacking those who say God speaks to them. Even some professing Christians have joined the crowd of skeptics. Recently a joyful Christian was asked incredulously, "You mean you hear God speak?" With a smile she replied, "You mean you don't?" If someone does not hear Jesus it could be because he does not belong to Him. For Jesus said, "My sheep hear My voice" (John 10:27).

Does this mean we should expect to hear an audible voice? No. It's much louder than that! For the sensitized Christian, the Spirit's inaudible voice in his spirit is much more pronounced than the voices of those around him.

While in past days we may have thought an ear tuned to heaven was valuable, in the future it will be vital. I believe we are entering an era where it will become increasingly vital for believers to live by revelation.

This is not to undercut the Bible in any way. I strongly believe in the inerrancy of Scripture. I do not believe, however, that God became mute and His people became deaf the day the Canon was closed. He is still speaking. And His people are still hearing.

We are at the changing of the guard. The torch of Christian leadership is being passed to a new generation. But it is not merely being transferred from older to younger. There is a new breed of leaders coming on the scene. The child Samuel could hear what the aging priest could not. There was an increase of perception.

Jesus pronounced loving yet firm warnings to His churches in Revelation 2 and 3. Then He said, "He who has an ear, let him hear what the Spirit says to the churches." In the midst of the Christian family's dirty laundry that has been exhibited gleefully by our critics, the Spirit is speaking again to the churches. For if we dismiss these difficult years as merely the devil's attack, I submit that we're not hearing very well. God wants the Church's attention. And once we're stilled before Him, He has plenty to say to us. "He who has an ear, let him hear."

Those who see the invisible and hear the inaudible will consequently *embrace the imperishable*. Look about you. Everything can be neatly placed into two categories: perishable and imperishable. Almost everything we see with physical eyes is in the first category. What about earth itself? Scripture teaches it will be purged with fire. How about wealth? It takes wings and flies away. Health, maybe? Not a chance. The outward man perishes. What about our expensive clothes? Not to mention the fact that they will soon be as out-of-style as button-up shoes, moths invade them. Cars? Rust corrodes them. Houses? Thieves break in and steal.

So what's left? Treasures in heaven. And these are not only inanimate things like crowns. The treasures are people themselves. Paul told the Thessalonian church, "For what is our hope, or joy, or crown of rejoicing? Is it not even you in the presence of our Lord Jesus Christ at His coming? For you are our glory and joy" (1 Thess. 2:19-20). What is our glory and joy? Not things — people. To have people we love with us in heaven — this is our hope, our joy, our crown of rejoicing. To embrace the imperishable is to embrace people.

And to embrace the imperishable is to embrace God. The highest of all rewards is to know God. God reminded Abram that He, not His blessings, was the great prize. "I am your shield, your exceedingly great reward" (Gen. 15:1). A right relationship to God and a right relationship to people — these are the greatest rewards in this life and the next.

Anointed to Serve

Again, it is the "other-worldly" who are best prepared to get this world's dirt under their nails and effect change. The heavenly minded are those uniquely anointed to serve their generation. Those who see the invisible, hear the inaudible, and embrace the imperishable can *do the impossible!* Spiritual perception requires faith. And without faith, almost everything is impossible, including being pleasing to

God (see Heb. 11:6). But Jesus said, "If you can believe, all things are possible to him who believes" (Mark 9:23).

> *Do you have faith to see the invisible? Will you believe to hear the inaudible? Have you chosen to embrace the imperishable? Then you are poised to do the impossible.*

Simple godly living, as demonstrated by the characteristics just mentioned, brings thrilling results. Not only will you be blessed, your offspring will be blessed. "He who fears the Lord has a secure fortress, and for his children it will be a refuge" (Prov. 14:26;NIV).

A godly life blesses society as well. This is vividly pictured in an interesting bit of research into the lives of two men, Max Jukes and Jonathan Edwards. Max Jukes was a vocal atheist who lived a godless life. He married an ungodly woman. Among the descendants of this union, 310 died as paupers, 150 were criminals, 7 were murderers, 100 were alcoholics, and more than half of the women were prostitutes. His 540 descendants cost the state one and a quarter million dollars.

During the same time that Max Jukes lived, there lived a great man of God, Jonathan Edwards. He married a godly woman. An investigation was made of the 1,394 known descendants of Jonathan Edwards. Thirteen became college presidents, 65 were college professors, 3 were United States senators, 30 were judges, 100 were lawyers, 60 were physicians, 75 were military officers, 100 were ministers and missionaries, 60 were authors, 1 was vice president of the United States, 80 were public officials in other capacities, and 295 were college graduates, among whom were governors of states and ambassadors to foreign countries. His descendants did not cost the government a penny.[2] "The memory of the righteous is blessed" (Prov. 10:7).

Jesus said that His followers are the salt of the earth. Salt may sting, but it also heals, preserves, and makes people thirsty. Our influence, though sometimes a sting to the open sores of society, should be a preservative and make people thirst for Jesus Christ, the Living Water.

As our gluttonous generation pursues selfish indulgence, it is also pleading, "Pass the salt!" As E.M. Bounds said, "We put it as our most sober judgment that the great need of the Church in this and all ages is men [and women] of such commanding faith, of such unsullied holiness, of such marked spiritual vigor and consuming zeal, that their prayers, faith, lives, and ministries will be of such a radical and aggressive form as to work spiritual revolutions which will form eras in individual and Church life."[3]

13

The Chemistry of the Universe

... God resists the proud, but gives grace to the humble. Therefore humble yourselves under the mighty hand of God, that He may exalt you in due time (1 Pet. 5:5-6).

Most of us probably remember the story of how Sir Walter Raleigh threw his cloak over a muddy puddle for the queen to walk on. His action was heralded as an act of chivalry. How noble that he would forego his expensive cloak for the good of the crown! But Sir Walter was nobody's fool. He knew that nothing is ever lost that is given to royalty. And when he sailed to the New World, he did not lack a powerful backer at home.

Likewise, that which we lay down for Jesus Christ is never lost. Fortunes may be laid down. Plans and dreams may be surrendered. Even lives may be sacrificed. But they are never lost. There is always an overwhelming recompense for anything we give to Him. God will be in no person's debt. That which is laid down for His majesty will be handsomely recompensed both in this life and afterward. And the more unselfishly we give, the more we become like Jesus.

St. Francis of Assisi understood this well. In a time of opulent indulgence in the Church, he took a voluntary vow of poverty. His simple lifestyle and innocent devotion to Christ were powerful rebukes to the greed that had engulfed Christendom. In his famous prayer to be an instrument of God's peace, St. Francis makes this observation: "It is in giving that we receive. It is in pardoning that we are pardoned. It is in dying that we are born to eternal life." In God's reversed scheme of things, those who win by intimidation lose everything and those who lose by self-giving win it all.

Let This Attitude Be in You

In the second chapter of Philippians Paul graphically details how Jesus emptied himself of His prerogatives as God. And Paul says we are to pour out our lives as well.

A beautiful picture of how our lives are to be thus given is seen in the old covenant drink offering. Once, during a battle in which the Philistines occupied Bethlehem, King David remarked that he longed for water from the well near Bethlehem's gate. Three of his mighty men immediately put their lives at risk, going behind enemy lines and retrieving the valued water for their king. Then David did something that, at first glance, might seem insane. Because the men had risked their lives, "David would not drink it, but poured it out to the Lord" (1 Chron. 11:18).

In the same way, our lives are valuable. We can indulge ourselves or we can pour our lives out as a drink offering to the Lord. But once again, that which is poured out is not lost. The costly offering is stored up in another world as a valuable investment in the afterlife.

To speak of laying down our lives, emptying and pouring them out, must sound shrill and foreign to the ears of many contemporary Christians. For we have been told that ours is a religion of receiving. And, of course, this is wonderfully true. I am not denying any of the rich benefits of our new covenant.

> *Mine is simply a voice — perhaps one of only a few right now — pleading that we see the other side of the coin. All Christianity is a religion of receiving. But mature Christianity is also a religion of sacrificial giving.*

After persecuting the Church before his conversion, Paul spent the rest of his life being spent for the Church and the advance of the gospel. Concerning his schedule that never let up, he commented, "If I am being poured out as a drink offering on the sacrifice and service of your faith, I am glad and rejoice with you all" (Phil. 2:17).

Paul had just rehearsed how Jesus himself was the prime example of what it means to be poured out. But because of His giving of himself — from heaven to a manger to a Cross — "God also has highly exalted Him and given Him the name which is above every name, that at the name of Jesus every knee should bow, of those in heaven, and of those on earth, and of those under the earth, and that every tongue should confess that Jesus Christ is Lord, to the glory of God the Father" (Phil. 2:9-11).

The chemistry of the universe has taken effect; humbling has brought exaltation.

Self-Worth and the Gospel

Many people today are so insecure they fear any self-sacrifice. People are as individual as snowflakes and every bit as fragile. Often they feel that their worth would be jeopardized by placing themselves in a vulnerable position of servanthood. Servants, after all, can be stepped on, despised, or worse yet, overlooked.

But it should be remembered that our intrinsic worth as humans has nothing to do with status. The emaciated Somalian is just as valuable as the head of a major corporation. The hunch-backed Indian who sweeps the floor all day with a whisk broom is just as valuable as the Hollywood movie star. Some may not really believe that, but God does. And it's His opinion that matters.

Communism is dehumanizing because it denies that people are made in the image of God. But capitalistic materialism also has its dehumanizing effects. We may laugh at the odd vocabulary of the California Valley Girl who says, "See, like, there's this guy, and, well, like, he drives a Jag." But ultimately it portrays a frightening inability in our society to separate the person from his possessions. People, no matter what they possess or do not possess, are valuable. And whether or not they are physically attractive, they are beautiful. Some of our simplest children's songs are amazingly profound: "Red, brown, yellow, black, and white — all are precious in His sight."

Our value as people is based on three important truths. First, we are valuable because we are made in the image of God. Like God, we can think, feel, and choose. Because we carry the image of our Creator, each person is infinitely precious. Consequently all human life is to be cherished and guarded, from conception until natural death.

Second, we are valuable because of the price paid for our redemption. As Dietrich Bonhoeffer said, "God's grace is free but it is not cheap." If ever you doubt your worth, look again at Calvary. And if ever you doubt that God loves you, look again at the dying Man on that cross. It is conceptually true that Jesus died for the world. But it is personally true that He died for you. His death touches you at the point of your need for love, acceptance, and forgiveness.

Third, we are valuable because each of us can make a unique contribution to the human experience. There is a circle of people you can reach that no one else can reach. Nobody can touch them quite like you. There may be a book in you no one else can write, a song no one else can compose, an affirmation no one else can offer, a discovery no one else can make. It belongs uniquely to you. And if you don't deliver, we will all be the poorer for it.

When these three simple truths become actual revelations inside you, you will have a foundation for inner security. Your identity crisis will be a thing of the past. Then you will be able to build on that foundation to even greater security as you discover more fully who you are in Christ.

Only the secure risk voluntary servitude. Yet only those who serve are truly fulfilled. Andrew Murray said, "Man's chief care, his highest virtue, and his only happiness, now and through eternity, is to present himself as an empty vessel in which God can dwell and manifest His power and goodness."[1]

Many serve behind the scenes so those on the front lines are free to give themselves to the battle. Most people cry at weddings. I tend to get misty-eyed at graduations. I know something of the sacrifice of parents and, yes, spouses and siblings to see their loved one in a cap and gown. And one day every faithful subordinate and trustworthy behind-the-scenes person will share in the reward of the ones out front. The Bible promises, "But as his part is who goes down to the battle, so shall his part be who stays by the supplies; they shall share alike" (1 Sam. 30:24).

Promotion's Source

The Bible says, "For exaltation comes neither from the east nor from the west nor from the south. But God is the Judge: He puts down one, and exalts another" (Ps. 75:6). Promotion is not a matter of being in the right place at the right time so the right guy can give you a break. Promotion comes from the Lord. And He always delights in lifting pure-hearted servants. "For the eyes of the Lord run to and fro throughout the whole earth, to show Himself strong on behalf of those whose heart is loyal to Him" (2 Chron. 16:9).

Yet the servant who realizes the dignity of his calling isn't really looking for promotion. He is looking for the Lord's nod of approval on his present assignment; that's all. He is content where he is, realizing that it is the Lord who has put him there. Andrew Murray had a deeper perception of servanthood than most. He said, "When we see that humility is something infinitely deeper than contrition, and accept it as our participation in the life of Jesus, we will begin to learn that it is our true nobility. We will begin to understand that being servants of all is the highest fulfillment of our destiny, as men created in the image of God."[2]

To allow the life of Christ to flow through our lives is the zenith of dignity. And when we allow His life to flow through ours, servanthood is the inevitable result. This is genuine success. Paul Rees observed, "If you want a picture of success as heaven measures it, of greatness as God views it, don't look for the blaring of the bands on Broadway; listen, rather, for the tinkle of water splashing into a basin, while God incarnate, in a humility that makes angels hold their breath, sponges the grime from the feet of His undeserving disciples."[3]

After Jesus performed this astonishing act, He endured the even greater indignity and demotion of stripping, torture, and death. But, little known to His human enemies and Satan himself, He was only hours away from ransacking hell of its captives and rising in resurrection splendor. His final step up was to the Father's right hand, "angels and authorities and powers having been made subject to Him" (1 Pet. 3:22).

Now we are called to follow in His steps of humility and servanthood. But, having done so, we will also follow in His cycle of victory and exaltation. It's the chemistry of the universe.

14

The Accountability Factor

For we must all appear before the judgment seat of Christ, that each one may receive what is due him for the things done while in the body, whether good or bad. Since, then, we know what it is to fear the Lord, we try to persuade men (2 Cor. 5:10-11;NIV).

The past several years have been rough for high visibility ministries. Close scrutiny from both friends and foes has uncovered some shocking and tragic revelations about immorality, infighting, and greed.

Heartbroken Christians, as well as outside sympathizers, are asking, "What's going on in the Church? How could this ever have happened?" The other day at the dentist's office, the dental assistant spoke for many when she asked me, "Isn't there *anybody* out there who's above reproach anymore?"

One conclusion everyone has come to is that no one is perfect. Of course, this is no grand revelation. It is merely a reiteration of Scripture's age-old teaching that all have sinned. But we must be careful not to take this admission too far. Instead of repenting of our sins and striving to live holy lives we seem to use our imperfection as a defense of indiscretion.

What *has* happened to us? What kind of climate has caused us to loosen our hold on morality? Of course, the answers are multiple and complex. But one shift in focus needs to be noted in particular. For the last several years we have tended to accept a no-accountability gospel. Sometimes it was preached in outright statements. At other times we arrived at that conclusion by inference. But it came out sounding something like, "Jesus has forgiven you. Your sins are covered. We live under grace." And beyond any question this is marvelously true. But the further message was "Therefore you are no longer accountable to God." And this is blatantly false.

Particularly popular among some of our leaders was a not-so-subtle message that, since they were anointed and chosen above the masses, God had somehow cut a special deal with them. God would give them a little more slack since His hand of blessing was clearly on them. And before we become angry at that kind of twisted reasoning, remember that good-hearted men like Samson, Saul, and David all bought into it. Far from getting off more lightly, James warns aspiring leaders, "My brethren, let not many of you become teachers, knowing that we shall receive a stricter judgment" (James 3:1).

Clearly, "the time has come for judgment to begin at the house of God" (1 Pet. 4:17). But before the mockers blast too harshly, let them remember the rest of that verse: "And if it begins with us first, what will be the end of those who do not obey the gospel of God?"

A New Call to Accountability

One hesitates to write or preach on accountability, particularly in the present climate. I, far better than any accusers, am acutely aware of my own struggles and deficiencies. Anyone who issues a fresh call to holiness feels like saying, with Paul, "Who is sufficient for these things?" (2 Cor. 2:16). I know all too well what lurks in my own heart. And the closer we get to God, the brighter is the spotlight of His searching purity. John Wesley, known as the great "holiness preacher," sensed his own fallibility. But he also recognized that his weaknesses did not cancel out God's truth. So he concluded, "I will preach holiness until I am holy. I will preach sanctification until I am sanctified."

God has clearly called us to a new sense of integrity and a new definition of success. Charles Malik, former secretary general of the United Nations, said before he died, "Success is neither fame, wealth, nor power; rather it is seeking, knowing, loving, and obeying God." By that standard, how many truly succeed?

It is our unaccountability message that has produced unaccountable people. And when people sense they are not accountable, their tainted natures throw off restraints. But Jesus reminds us, "For there is nothing hidden which will not be revealed, nor has anything been kept secret but that it should come to light" (Mark 4:22). Now, was Jesus speaking metaphorically or did He actually mean that? And, if you were a betting person, how much would you wager against a literal interpretation?

> *If we take what He said at face value (and there is no reason not to do so), nothing hidden or secret will stay that way. If that is true, investigative reporters are the least of our concerns. The Holy Spirit himself is doing His own investigation. And He will hold us fully accountable.*

Knowing our own proclivity to sin, then, we must flee to the investigator as the exonerator. The same Spirit who brings our sins to light gives us power over them.

"Before Jesus" in Relationships

A man who is now a noted preacher tells how his Christian parents taught him to tell the truth when he was a little boy. Having stolen cookies from the cookie jar, he tried to hide his guilt. "Son," his parents inquired, "did you take any cookies?"

Poker-faced, he replied, "No. I didn't."

Then his folks restated the question. "Son, *before Jesus*, did you take any cookies from the jar?"

The boy gulped and replied, "Well, if you put it that way, I did."

Everything in our lives is before Jesus. We need to remember that, especially in the area of relationships. We are prone to treat people as expendable objects rather than the crowning glory of God's creation. Corrie Ten Boom said, "Every experience God gives us, every person He puts in our lives, is the perfect preparation for the future that only He can see." No one comes into your life by accident. They are there either for you to minister to them or for them to minister to you. There is, as Corrie reminded us, some purpose yet unseen that brings lives together.

The concept of acting honorably is, perhaps, most ignored in our relationships with the opposite sex. There is often little difference between the moral conduct of Christians and non-Christians. Many who profess faith in Christ have bought into the same rationales for permissiveness as unbelievers. Not only is this flirting with fire, it is courting moral and spiritual disaster. Elisabeth Elliot cogently battles this loose thinking:

> Christians who are buying such rubbish today are without honor. They have lost the notions of fidelity, renunciation, and sacrifice, because nothing seems worth all that.

There is nothing for which they will pay the price of actual, conscious, painful, down-to-earth self-denial — except (and I am convinced this is a significant exception) visible gains like money and sports. If young people have heroes today, they are athletes. If they have role models of endurance and sacrifice and self-discipline, they are athletes. If a man denies himself comforts, vacations, pleasures with his family, evenings at home, or the free indulgence of whatever appetite he feels, it is usually for money. Nobody will worry very much about his being repressive or fanatical or weird, so long as money is his motive.

If your goal is purity of heart, be prepared to be thought very odd.[1]

Powerful words. Let us remember that there is a visible gain for purity of heart; it just isn't seen in this sphere. Visible, tangible awards await the pure.

"Before Jesus" in Stewardship of Finances

The Bible clearly commands us not to labor for the purpose of becoming rich. Yet vast numbers are racing at breakneck speed as workaholics, trying to secure financially the very families they are losing through overwork. But if we do not work for the purpose of money, why work at all?

For one thing, work itself is honorable. God blesses human labor. Indeed it can be an act of worship to offer our work to God.

In exchange for the investment of our time — which really constitutes our lives — we are given money. What the Christian does with that money, he should remember, is "before Jesus." God is observing what we do with His tender.

152 • Ultimate Success

It is honorable to meet our financial obligations. Failure to do so brings reproach on the name of Christ. It is honorable to invest for the future, give to the needy, make our families secure, and spontaneously allow money to do what it can do in alleviating suffering and advancing the gospel.

It is not necessarily honorable to give a tenth of our incomes back to God. Tithing is simply required. As we obey the Spirit's promptings to give above the tithe, *that* is honorable.

Jerry Cook, West Coast pastor and author, gives a beautiful illustration of a genuinely Christian heart of giving: "I've been to the highlands of New Guinea, where people live in abject poverty. One day my host took me into the countryside and said, 'Pick out the Christians' gardens.' I looked and sure enough, the gardens of the believers were producing better than those of the non-believers. 'We pray over our gardens,' my host explained. 'We want to grow enough food to share with our neighbors who cannot pray God's blessings on their gardens as we do.' "[2] That kind of heart will not go unrewarded.

The side of town one lives on or the kind of vehicle he drives is really not the issue. As Pastor Cook reminds us. "What I'm doing with my resources says infinitely more about my spiritual condition than does the fact that I have them."[3]

"Before Jesus" in Investment of Time

Perhaps the best barometer of our true spiritual condition is how we use our free time. One-third of our time is already spoken for in work. Another third we give to sleep. But that leaves approximately *eight hours each day* to invest as we wish. Whether we admit it or not, most of us end up doing pretty much what we want to do most of the time.

Time can be spent or it can be invested. Clear priorities should mark our use of time. First and foremost, we should give time to God. This sets the tone for any other expenditure of time. We will not be at our best, emotionally or otherwise, if we have not given time to this relationship.

Then we should give high priority to our families. No relationship can be nurtured without the investment of time. Frightening statistics have emerged concerning the amount of actual time spent among parents and children. No doubt the same is true for spouses. Time is the soil into which we sow our love and concern. If little is sown, there will be little harvest.

We are also to invest time with our extended family, the church. And even beyond our local church, we are to give time and care to the entire body of Christ. The Bible teaches we are to do good to everyone, but especially to those who are of the household of faith (see Gal. 6:10).

But we must also reserve time to invest in God's purposes in our generation. For some, this will involve a change of career or relocation in a present career, becoming a sort of tentmaker missionary like Paul. Volunteer work in community projects, vacation time used for short-term missions projects, visitation in hospitals and rest homes — these should also be prayerfully included on the Christian's agenda.

The point of all of this is that we're accountable for how we live. With our relationships, our money, our time, we are living our days before Jesus.

────15────

A Theology of Hope

*Blessed be the God and Father of our Lord
Jesus Christ, who according to His abundant
mercy has begotten us again to a living hope
through the resurrection of Jesus Christ from
the dead, to an inheritance incorruptible and
undefiled and that does not fade away, reserved in heaven for you* (1 Pet. 1:3-4).

Have you ever wondered why new Christians seem
invariably drawn to the Book of Revelation? This has
always intrigued me. Several times I've urged a new believer to begin reading his Bible, starting with John or
Romans, only to have him ask, "But what about that book at
the back of the Bible?" Why are they so intrigued with
Revelation?

Some years back, Pastor Jerry Cook asked the same
question. He relates how he thought the devil was trying to
confuse new believers, by drowning them in charts, dates,
numerology, and questions about beasts and dragons. Why
this desire to read Revelation? Then a thought came to him:
Don't you think that desire may be born of the Holy Spirit?

The Lord impressed this pastor simply to read the Book of Revelation to his congregation and cautioned him, *Don't you dare do an exposition on it.* Pastor Cook relates what happened.

> We simply read Revelation. When we got through, we had a phenomenal concept of the *power of Jesus,* of the *sovereignty of God,* of the *security that is ours* on this planet, and of the utter, complete, unquestionable *triumph of the church* of Jesus Christ. On that last night the congregation stood together with uplifted hands and praised the Lord for nearly half an hour. I've never seen anything so powerful in all my life. I thought, *That's why the Lord takes new Christians to the Book of Revelation. What does a new Christian need to know more than those four things?*[1]

Unspeakable pain can be endured provided we have inside information regarding the ultimate outcome. Job was deprived of wealth, position, health, and family — all in one day. His pain was augmented by heartless "comforters" and an unsupportive, bitter companion. Those who have experienced heartache and reversal (and that will probably be everyone who picks up this book) can learn from Job's response in the midst of disaster.

What is left of faith when it is distilled to its essence? Job, having been stripped of all he held dear was left with a no-nonsense, no-hype faith. Yet, after the devil had done his worst, Job maintained a theology of hope. After his compounded tragedies he made a ringing confession of faith. He declared, "For I know that my Redeemer lives, and He shall stand at last on the earth; and after my skin is destroyed, this I know, that in my flesh I shall see God" (Job 19:25-26).

Job knew he had a living Redeemer who would one day

stand on the earth in final triumph. He saw beyond his present pain to a day free of suffering. He also knew that he would experience a physical resurrection. "In my flesh," he said, "I shall see God." The eternal destiny of his body was not corruption but glorification.

No trial is too difficult if we really know that, when all is said and done, we will see God and He will see us. This is to retain a theology of hope.

Perhaps, like Job, you live in an environment that is hostile to your faith in a living Redeemer. Your friends may be less than supportive. There may be angry denunciations of your stand within your own family. You may have been pelted all at once with hell's heaviest arsenals. At such a time, when faith is boiled down to what you know without question, your heart can still hold confident assurance. You still have a triumphant, living Redeemer. He will write the final chapter. And, in a body fit for eternal habitation with Him, you will see God.

An Anchor for the Soul

The events of the last few years seem to indicate that we have embarked on the final shaking prophesied in Hebrews. This shaking is so "that the things which cannot be shaken may remain" (Heb. 12:27). It is a time of violent tossing as hurricane winds of doubt, hurt, and lost confidence are blasting away at the faith of millions. Seemingly everything we possess, spiritually and emotionally, that's not bolted down is being blown away.

In light of these conditions, how should we then live? After announcing this time of shaking, the writer of Hebrews exhorts us to a distinctive standard of living. "Therefore, since we are receiving a kingdom which cannot be shaken, let us have grace, by which we may serve God acceptably with reverence and godly fear" (Heb. 12:28). Notice that we are not merely to serve God, we are to serve Him in an acceptable fashion. Reverence for God is always the climate that produces acceptable service.

But notice, too, that this acceptable service is predicated on the sure assumption that we are headed for an unshakable Kingdom. Much of the world is sinking deeper into the phobia and Chicken Little hysteria that "the sky is falling in." Things (and people) once thought impeccably secure are being ripped from their hinges. Many believers are being "tossed to and fro and carried about with every wind of doctrine" (Eph. 4:14). In a world gone mad, what on earth *abides*?

The essence of Christian experience abides, transcending the erosion of time and the blasts of its enemies. What is this essence? Faith, hope, and love. It is true that Satan has targeted these essential components. He attacks faith by trying to make us skeptical. He aims at love by attempting to make us critical. And he fires at hope by trying to make us cynical. Nevertheless, these components remain. "And now abide faith, hope, love . . ." (1 Cor. 13:13).

The character of God also remains unchanged. "His compassions fail not. They are new every morning; great is Your faithfulness" (Lam. 3:22-23). God has entered into a covenant oath of love with His people. He has promised never to leave or forsake us (see Heb. 13:5). And, since it is impossible for God to lie, Scripture says we have a strong consolation (see Heb. 6:18).

Certainly not least in our core of unshakable things is our confidence of heaven and all it contains. The return of Christ is the blessed hope of the believer. And the sure prospect of an eternity with Him drives us back to steadiness when the winds blow. In the midst of hell's bombardments, there is assurance of victory for those "who have fled for refuge to lay hold of the hope set before us. This hope we have as an anchor of the soul, both sure and steadfast . . ." (Heb. 6:18-19).

No greater gift could be given you than the assurance of a future, a certain "hope which is laid up for you in heaven" (Col. 1:5). Even your present trials are pregnant with hope because He lives. You have been born again, not to a death wish, but to a living, confident hope.

An Inevitably Brighter Tomorrow

> *Alexander Pope said, "Hope springs eternal in the human breast." Believers do not "hope in hope," we hope in the living God. Hope does indeed spring eternal in the hearts of those who think and live from a perspective that is eternal.*

This allows us to smile amid tragedy and live steadily amid disaster. Jeremiah had watched his nation be pillaged methodically by ruthless enemies. Yet, in the throes of national defeat and personal anguish, he worshipped God for His faithfulness, declaring, "Your compassions fail not."

The majestic hymn "Now Thank We All Our God" was written by Martin Rinkhart during the Thirty Years' War of 1618-1648, while he was pastor at Eilenburg in Saxony. The little town was severely attacked three times yet it served as a haven for refugees. There was intense famine and pestilence. For some time Rinkhart was the only pastor in the city, and during the great pestilence of 1637 he conducted about 4,500 burial services — sometimes as many as 40 or 50 a day. In the midst of these horrendous circumstances, he wrote these lines of thanksgiving to God:

> *Now thank we all our God with hearts and
>   hands and voices,*
> *Who wondrous things hath done, in whom
>   His world rejoices;*
> *Who from our mothers' arms hast blest us on
>   our way*
> *With countless gifts of love, and still is ours
>   today.*

Because we see beyond the present to an eternally wonderful future, we stay steady in adversity. Pain is temporary — heaven's rest is eternal.

Just think of it. The Bible teaches we will "sit down with Abraham, Isaac, and Jacob in the kingdom of heaven" (Matt. 8:11). Already, the saints of previous ages are discussing not only their past accomplishments, but the present Church's possibilities. A family friend was declared clinically dead for several hours and had an out-of-the-body experience. He described, as best he could, what he saw as he was transported to heaven. Of particular interest to me was how he saw my father, who was a great missions enthusiast, and David Livingstone engaged in joyful conversation. No doubt, their subject was world evangelization — not in their generations, but in this one.

As we have seen, the Church is never diminished by the death of its members. Earthbound believers enjoy a "mystic, sweet communion with those whose race is won." Those who truly know Jesus Christ as Saviour and Lord are simply re-stationed for another assignment. Disappointments are for them a thing of the past. If you know Jesus, there is an inevitably brighter tomorrow. The Church's one foundation, now, then and always is Jesus Christ. Even in the midst of our indefensible shortcomings, He will lead His church to ultimate victory. Christ's redeemed are destined for the throne, to reign with Him.

> *Mid toil and tribulation and tumult of her war,*
> *She waits the consummation of peace forevermore;*
> *Till with the vision glorious her longing eyes are blest,*
> *And the great church victorious shall be the church at rest.*[2]

"God Shall Wipe Away All Tears . . . ."

J.H. Thornwell said, "If the Church could be aroused to a deeper sense of the glory that awaits her, she would enter with a warmer spirit into the struggles that are before her." That's what I've attempted to do in these pages — arouse us as Christians to a deeper sense of the glories that await us. Thus strengthened, we are equipped for victory in our present struggles.

Paul prayed that Ephesian believers might be given "the spirit of wisdom and revelation in the knowledge of Him, the eyes of your understanding being enlightened; that you may know what is the hope of His calling, what are the riches of the glory of His inheritance in the saints" (Eph. 1:17-18). A greater revelation of our future gives us a clearer perception of our present. A greater revelation of Christ brings a clearer understanding and assurance of our calling in His grace.

Twice in Revelation we are told that God will wipe away all tears (Rev. 7:17; 21:4). When we get to heaven we will be far more acutely aware of our lost time and lost opportunities. For many, the response will be tears of regret. And for all of us there will be, no doubt, one final burst of emotional release that brings total healing. In ministry to the hurting, I've witnessed that, just prior to a deep work of inner restoration, there is often an outburst of crying. Just so, our tears of remorse, regret, and release will be washed away in the sea of His firm, tender love on That Day.

You may be in the thick of confusing conflicts, even now. The thermostat of affliction may have been turned up higher. If so, there are three simple assurances you need to recall.

First, *Jesus Christ is going to win.* Every knee will one day bow to Him. Every human, angelic, and demonic tongue will confess, "Jesus Christ is Lord." The present struggles for world domination will have no effect on the final outcome. The battle for this planet is fixed! Jesus shall reign.

Second, *you are going to win.* If you have been bought with Jesus' blood, He has an enormous vested interest in you. Absolutely nothing in your past, present, or future can sever you from His love. He has taken you on as a lifetime project. And He has vowed to finish in you what He has started.

Third, *the Church is going to win.* The present convulsions, attacks, and apparent recessions are temporary. World evangelization will one day be more than a distant dream, it will be a realized hope. Not only will heaven ring with His praise, "the earth shall be full of the knowledge of the Lord as the waters cover the sea" (Isa. 11:9). You're on the winning team.

> *Though the cause of evil prosper,*
> *Yet 'tis truth alone is strong;*
> *Though her portion be the scaffold,*
> *And upon the throne be wrong,*
> *Yet that scaffold sways the future,*
> *And, behind the dim unknown,*
> *Standeth God within the shadow*
> *Keeping watch above his own.*[3]

A Closing Word

Some time back a delegation of American business-men witnessed Mother Teresa's work in Calcutta. They observed her incessant ministry to some of the world's most neglected: the malnourished, the abject poor, and the termi-nally ill. As she compassionately dressed the open wounds of a leper, one of the party recoiled in revulsion. "I wouldn't do that for a million dollars!" he exclaimed.

Looking up, Mother Teresa smiled and answered, "Neither would I." To a large extent our motives determine our actions. And the purer the motives, the greater the rewards. "Blessed are the pure in heart, for they shall see God" (Matt. 5:8).

"Genuine success," as George Truett often said, "is to know the will of God and do it." As Paul approached death he rejoiced that he had completed his course. He had long desired a joyful conclusion to the ministry he had received from the Lord.

You, as well, have received a ministry. The faithful execution of that work He has put in your hands constitutes a truly successful life. And such a life prepares you for rewards in heaven and advanced status in Christ's new order when He reigns over the earth.

I've been privileged to meet some godly giants of the

past in the latter years of their lives here: men like Paul Billheimer, David du Plessis, R.G. Lee, J. Edwin Orr, and Oswald J. Smith. Each of these men was renowned and revered in his day. Yet each of them lived to see an age when the Christian public, though continuing to venerate them, bypassed them for younger, flashier leaders. I cannot say that I was close to any of these men. My encounters with them were few and brief, but each of them marked my life. They shared one common trait: they all seemed so conscious of heaven, so in touch with another world.

Heaven's signals are often silenced amid today's clamor. But those who mark their world, as Thoreau reminds us, are those who hear and march to a different drummer. To adopt heaven's values is to live for what matters. And what matters are those very few, highly precious things we can take with us into the afterlife.

We will travel light when we finally go home — our baggage will consist of souls we have brought to Christ and the intimacy with God we've developed. (Perhaps this is why my wife's grandmother continued to take Moody Bible Institute correspondence courses well into her nineties. She wanted to know more about the Lord she would soon meet face to face.) That's it. That's all the baggage this flight, not through time zones but through light years, will allow. But we can transfer vast amounts of earth's currency and commodities into heaven's tender. We can send a great deal on ahead, in preparation for our coming.

To divest oneself of rusting riches now for timeless treasures then is only prudent. As Jim Elliot said, "That man is no fool who gives up that which he cannot keep to gain that which he cannot lose." You will never regret living these days in light of That Day. And you would sorely regret *not* doing so.

All of us have a long way to go toward Christlikeness. Someone said, "I won't arrive until He arrives." Nevertheless, we keep pressing toward the goal of conformity to Him.

"Brethren, I do not count myself to have apprehended; but one thing I do, forgetting those things which are behind and reaching forward to those things which are ahead, I press toward the goal for the prize of the upward call of God in Christ Jesus" (Phil. 3:13-14).

As we run for the prize the distractions are legion: the weights of life, easily besetting sins, and the taunts and jeers of those already sidelined. The best insurance that you will finish honorably is to stop your ears to the heckling of the critics and the pleadings of your own flesh and fix your eyes, your heart, your total energies on the goal.

And as you run, be encouraged by the words of a dying prophet who caught a glimpse of the victory celebration on the other side of the tape. "The best of all is, God is with us!"

NOTES

Chapter 1

[1]Judson Cornwall, *Heaven* (Van Nuys, CA: Bible Voice, 1978), p. 25.

[2]E.M. Bounds, *Catching a Glimpse of Heaven* (Springdale, PA: Whitaker House, 1985), p. 98.

[3]Charles C. Luther, (1847-1924), "Must I Go, and Empty-Handed?"

[4]William J. Reynolds, *Companion to the Baptist Hymnal* (Nashville, TN: Broadman Press, 1976), p. 183.

[5]Alexander Solzhenitsyn, *Gulag Archipelago II* (New York, NY: Harper & Row, 1975), p. 615.

[6]A.W. Tozer, *The Pursuit of God* (Harrisburg, PA: Christian Publications, 1982), p. 113.

[7]Edward Mote, "The Solid Rock" (1832).

Chapter 2

[1]William Shakespeare, *As You Like It*, II, vii.

[2]Philip Yancey, "Heaven Can't Wait," *Christianity Today* (September 7, 1984), p. 53.

[3]John Braun, *Whatever Happened to Hell?* (Nashville, TN: Thomas Nelson, 1979), p. 105-106.

[4]Oswald Chambers, *My Utmost for His Highest* (New York, NY: Dodd, Mead & Co., 1935), p. 335.

[5]Quoted by Malcolm Muggeridge, *A Twentieth Century Testimony* (Nashville, TN: Thomas Nelson, 1978), p. 16.

Chapter 3

[1]Betty Malz, *My Glimpse of Eternity* (Old Tappan, NJ: Chosen Books, 1977), p. 86-88.

[2]Cornwall, *Heaven.* I have relied heavily on the research of Judson Cornwall in this area, particularly from chapter 5 of this book.

[3]Joseph Bayly, "What Heaven Will Be Like," *Moody Monthly* (May 1976), p. 27.

[4]David Watson, *Fear No Evil* (London: Hodder & Stoughton, 1984), p. 166-167.

[5]C.S. Lewis, *Mere Christianity* (New York, NY: Macmillan, 1943), p. 118.

[6]Bishop Augustine and others, *The City of God* (New York, NY: Doubleday Co., 1979).

[7]Edith Schaeffer, *Christianity Today* (March 12, 1976), p. 41.

[8]C.S. Lewis, *The Problem of Pain* (Glasgow: William Collins Sons & Co., Ltd., 1940), p. 115.

Chapter 4

[1]Cornwall, *Heaven*, p. 54.

[2]James Matthew Barrie, *The Twelve Pound Book*, listed in *Bartlett's Familiar Quotations* (Boston, MA: Little, Brown, 1968), p. 858.

[3]Robert Browning, "The Last Ride Together."

[4]Alexander Pope, *An Essay on Man,* Espistle II.

Chapter 5

[1]Betty Lee Skinner, *Daws* (Grand Rapids, MI: Zondervan Publishing House, 1974), p. 190, 350.

Chapter 7

[1]H.L. Mencken, *A New Dictionary of Quotations* (New York, NY: Alfred A. Knopf, 1966), p. 527.

[2]Watson, *Fear No Evil*, p. 164.

[3]Horatio G. Spafford, "It Is Well with My Soul" (1873).

[4]Herbert Lockyer, *Last Words of Saints and Sinners* (Grand Rapids, MI: Kregel Publications, 1969), p. 114.

Chapter 9

[1]Andrew Murray, *Humility* (Springdale, PA: Whitaker House, 1982), p. 10.

Chapter 10

[1]W.E. Vine, *Vine's Expository Dictionary of New Testament Words* (Lynchburg, VA: Old-Time Gospel Hour), p. 250. See Revelation 19:12, 16.

Chapter 11

[1]Quoted by Dick Eastman, *The Hour that Changes the World* (Grand Rapids, MI: Baker, 1978), p. 48.

[2]Tim LaHaye, *Life in the Afterlife* (Wheaton, IL: Tyndale House, 1980), p. 69.

Chapter 12

[1] I am indebted to Dr. Howard Ervin for the insight concerning the relationship between quantum mechanics and theology.

[2] Leonard Ravenhill, *America Is Too Young to Die* (Minneapolis, MN: Bethany Fellowship, 1979), p. 112.

[3] E.M. Bounds, *Power through Prayer* (Chicago, IL: Moody Press, 1979), p. 94.

Chapter 13

[1] Murray, *Humililty*, p. 10.

[2] Murray, *Humility*, p. 7.

[3] Paul Rees, quoted in *Encyclopedia of 7700 Illustrations* (Rockville, MD: Assurance Publishers, 1979), p. 1371-1372.

Chapter 14

[1] Elisabeth Elliot, *Passion and Purity* (Old Tappan, NJ: Fleming H. Revell Co., 1984), p. 129-130.

[2] Jerry Cook, *Love, Acceptance & Forgiveness* (Glendale, CA: Regal Books, 1979), p. 125.

[3] Cook, *Love, Acceptance & Forgiveness*, p. 125.

Chapter 15

[1] Cook, *Love, Acceptance & Forgiveness*, p. 63.

[2] Samuel J. Stone, "The Church's One Foundation" (1866).

[3] James Russell Lowell, "Once to Every Man and Nation" (1845).

Scripture Study

What the Bible says about . . .

Personal Accountability to God

Genesis 12:2
Amos 4:12
Mark 4:22
Romans 14:11-12
1 Corinthians 4:5
Colossians 3:22-25
Hebrews 12:28-29

Psalm 24:1
Matthew 5:21
Acts 17:30-31
1 Corinthians 3:11-15
2 Corinthians 5:10
2 Thessalonians 1:7-10
Jude 24-25

Entrance Into Heaven

John 1:11-12
John 3:16
Ephesians 2:8-9

John 3:3
Romans 10:9-10, 13

Eternal Rewards

2 Chronicles 16:9
Psalm 126:5-6
Isaiah 40:10
Hosea 10:12
Matthew 10:41-42
Matthew 25:21
Mark 10:29-30
Luke 12:42-44
Romans 12:19
1 Corinthians 3:14
Galatians 6:7-9
Ephesians 6:5-8
Colossians 1:5
1 Timothy 4:8
Hebrews 10:34-35
Hebrews 11:24-26
James 1:12
1 Peter 4:12-13

Psalm 58:11
Proverbs 11:18
Daniel 12:3
Matthew 5:3-12
Matthew 16:27
Mark 9:41
Luke 6:35, 38
John 12:26
1 Corinthians 2:9
1 Corinthians 9:25
Ephesians 2:7
Philippians 3:13-14
1 Thessalonians 2:19-20
2 Timothy 4:7-8
Hebrews 11:6
Hebrews 12:1-3
1 Peter 1:3-7
1 Peter 5:1-4

2 Peter 1:5-11
2 John 8
Revelation 3:11

1 John 3:2-3
Revelation 2:10
Revelation 22:12

Victory Over Death

Psalm 23:4
Psalm 116:15
1 Corinthians 15:53-58
Hebrews 2:14-15
Revelation 21:4

Psalm 30:5
Proverbs 10:7
2 Corinthians 5:1-2, 8
Revelation 1:18

Gaining An Eternal Perspective

Psalm 139:23-24
Luke 12:33
John 17:3
1 Corinthians 13:13
2 Corinthians 4:16-18
Philippians 3:20-21
Hebrews 13:14

Matthew 6:19-21
John 3:16
Romans 8:28-29
1 Corinthians 15:19
Philippians 1:6
Colossians 3:1-2
James 4:14

This is not an exhaustive list of Scriptures related to these topics. Rather, they represent a sample of the Bible's extensive treatment of each of these subjects.

Bibliography

Billheimer, Paul. *Destined for the Throne*. Fort Washington, PA: Christian Literature Crusade, 1975.

Billheimer, Paul. *Destined to Overcome*. Fort Washington, PA: Christian Literature Crusade, 1982.

Billheimer, Paul. *Don't Waste Your Sorrows*. Fort Washington, PA: Christian Literature Crusade, 1977.

Bounds, E.M. *Catching a Glimpse of Heaven*. Springdale, PA: Whitaker House, 1985.

Braun, John. *Whatever Happened to Hell?* Nashville, TN: Thomas Nelson, 1979.

Chambers, Oswald. *My Utmost for His Highest*. New York, NY: Dodd, Mead & Company, 1935.

Colson, Charles. *Loving God*. Grand Rapids, MI: Judith Markham/ Zondervan, 1983.

Cornwall, Judson. *Heaven*. Van Nuys, CA: Bible Voice, 1978.

Eastman, Dick. *The Hour that Changes the World*. Grand Rapids, MI: Baker, 1978.

Eby, Richard E. *Caught Up into Paradise*. LaVerne, CA: El Camino Press.

Elliot, Elisabeth. *Passion and Purity*. Old Tappan, NJ: Revell, 1984.

Foster, Richard J. *Money, Sex & Power*. New York, NY: Harper & Row, 1985.

Fuller, Daniel P. *Give the Winds a Mighty Voice*. Waco, TX: Word, 1972.

Gillquist, Peter E. *Designed for Holiness*. Ann Arbor, MI: Servant, 1986.

Graham, Billy. *Angels: God's Secret Agents.* Garden City, NY: Doubleday, 1975.

Graham, Billy. *Facing Death and the Life After.* Waco, TX: Word, 1987.

Graham, Billy. *Approaching Hoofbeats,* Waco, TX: Word, 1983.

Greene, Oliver B. *Heaven.* Greenville, SC: The Gospel Hour, 1969.

Gundry, Stanley & Patricia. *The Wit and Wisdom of D. L. Moody.* Chicago, IL: Moody, 1974.

Kirban, Salem. *How to Be Sure of Crowns in Heaven.* Huntingdon Valley, PA: Salem Kirban, Inc., 1981.

LaHaye, Tim. *Life in the Afterlife.* Wheaton, IL: Tyndale House, 1980.

Lewis, C.S. *The Great Divorce.* Glasgow: William Collins Sons & Co., Ltd., 1946, 1972.

Lewis, C.S. *The Joyful Christian.* New York, NY: Macmillan, 1977.

Lewis, C.S. *The Problem of Pain.* Glasgow: William Collins Sons & Co., Ltd., 1940, 1957.

Malz, Betty. *Angels Watching over Me.* Old Tappan, NJ: Chosen Books, 1986.

Malz, Betty. *My Glimpse of Eternity.* Old Tappan, NJ: Chosen Books, 1977.

McKee, Bill. *Order Your Crowns Now.* Nashville, TN: Impact/ Benson, 1976.

Muggeridge, Malcolm. *A Twentieth Century Testimony.* Nashville, TN: Thomas Nelson, 1978.

Murray, Andrew. *Humility.* Springdale, PA: Whitaker House, 1982.

Myers, John. *Voices from the Edge of Eternity.* Old Tappan, NJ: Spire/Revell, 1968.

Rice, John R. *Bible Facts About Heaven.* Murfeesboro, TN: Sword of the Lord, 1940.

Rice, Max M. *Your Rewards in Heaven.* Denver, CO: Accent, 1981.

Richardson, Don. *Eternity in their Hearts.* Glendale, CA: Regal, 1981.

Rinehart, Stacy & Paula. *Living in Light of Eternity.* Colorado Springs, CO: NavPress, 1986.

Schaeffer, Edith. *A Way of Seeing.* Old Tappan, NJ: Revell, 1977.

Shibley, David. *When Your Dream's Don't Come True.* Green Forest, AR: New Leaf Press, 1993.

Shibley, David. *Now That You Are His.* Green Forest, AR: New Leaf Press, 1993.

Skinner, Betty Lee. *Daws.* Grand Rapids, MI: Zondervan Publishing House, 1974.

Spurgeon, C.H. *Sermons.* Second Series. New York, NY: Robert Carter & Brothers, 1857.

Tozer, A.W. *The Pursuit of God.* Harrisburg, PA: Christian Publications, Inc.

Vanauken, Sheldon. *A Severe Mercy.* New York, NY: Harper & Row, 1977.

Vine, W.E. *An Expository Dictionary of New Testament Words.* Lynchburg, VA: The Old Time Gospel Hour.

Watson, David. *Fear No Evil.* London: Hodder & Stoughton, 1984.

Wuest, Kenneth S. *First Peter in the Greek New Testament.* Grand Rapids, MI: Wm. B Eerdmans, 1942.

David Shibley

David Shibley is president and founder of Global Advance, a missions ministry equipping and resourcing national church leaders to reach people with the gospel. With over a quarter century of fruitful ministry, he has ministered in over 30 nations. Also, he travels extensively throughout the United States, speaking in behalf of world evangelization.

Mr. Shibley knows what works from a lifetime of missions involvement. A clear vision has emerged in his heart to quickly, sensitively, and cost-effectively fulfill Christ's Great Commission. The key lies with national church leaders — frontline shepherds. Global Advance equips these leaders for world harvest through Frontline Shepherds Conferences in many nations. These strategic leaders leave with a vision in their hearts and tools in their hands.

In addition to his ministry with Global Advance, Mr. Shibley serves on eight mission boards and is a member of the far-reaching U.S. Lausanne Committee on World Evangelization. He is the author of eight books and numerous articles.

A graduate of John Brown University in Arkansas, and Southwestern Baptist Theological Seminary, he holds an honorary doctorate from ORU. He and his wife, Naomi, have two sons.

For more information regarding the ministry of Global Advance and David Shibley, contact:

Global Advance
P.O. Box 742077
Dallas, TX 75087-0222

(214) 771-9042
FAX (214) 722-6119

Other books by David Shibley

What to Do
When Your Dreams Don't Come True
Starting over after life's disappointments

When you are forced by circumstances or detours to wait a long time, you may think a dream will never come true. Here is healing and spiritual refreshment when hopes have been crushed. You can recapture your vision and run toward the future!

In this timely book you will discover:

- How dreams sometimes must die so that destiny can live.
- Major barriers to the realization of dreams.
- God's purpose for allowing failure or disappointment.
- How to find joy in the midst of pain and heartbreak.

$7.95

Now That You Are His
First Steps in the Christian Walk

You have made a commitment of your life to Christ as Lord and Saviour. Now that you are His, you can take the following specific steps to help you grow as a Christian:

- publicly confessing your faith in Christ,
- being baptized in water,
- fellowshipping with others in a strong local church,
- getting the foundation right,
- being grounded in God's Word,
- dev~' ng a dynamic prayer life,
  others for Jesus,
  d's promises.

set you on the path of a fruitful life in

bookstores nationwide
1-800-643-9535